D0880850

CASSEROLE SPECIALTIES

Also by Nedda Casson Anders

CHAFING-DISH SPECIALTIES

ROASTER-OVEN COOKBOOK

COMPLETE COOKBOOK FOR BROILER AND ROTISSERIE

CASSEROLE SPECIALTIES

Nedda Casson Anders

GRAMERCY PUBLISHING COMPANY • NEW YORK

This edition published by Gramercy Publishing Company,
a division of Crown Publishers, Inc.,
by arrangement with Hearthside Press, Inc.

L M N O P Q R S

Contents

ALL ABOUT CASSEROLE COOKING

How to select casseroles : What size casserole? : Hints for buffet parties : My favorite French dressing : A basic medium white sauce : How to freeze casseroles

In ovens all over America, casseroles of every size and shape are baking succulent meals for the family, for neighbors in for a Saturday social, and for special guests in whose honor we set our daintiest china and finest crystal. Casseroles are universally appealing. They are easy to prepare and delicious as only oven-baked food can be. Because they have stayability, hostesses find dinner can await a tardy guest, another round of cocktails, and the end of a long rubber of bridge. Is it any wonder that women have rediscovered the pleasures of casserole cooking?

Here in these pages are recipes for casserole *specialties*—interesting and different meal-in-one combinations that are a culinary heritage from the Greeks, Germans, Scandinavians, the Russians, Armenians, Italians, the Spaniards, Jews, and Chinese. You will find such international favorites as Paella, Lasagne, and Boo Loo Gai, such popular American regional casseroles as Jumbalaya and Deep-Dish Ham and Apple Pie.

With each recipe is a menu—not necessarily an authentic import—but an American version suited to our tastes and preferences. Because most casseroles are of the hearty type, very often only a green salad, hot rolls, coffee and perhaps a simple dessert are suggested. Sometimes there are casserole desserts to bake along with the main dish. More often the desserts do not require cooking. After all, one of the special qualities of casserole meals is ease of preparation, so let's put our best efforts into the main dish and serve such satisfying and quick desserts as vanilla ice cream with crushed roast peanuts, or whole strawberries marinated in Kirsch liqueur, or fresh figs in heavy cream. Or just a bowl or basket or tray of fruits in season.

how to select casseroles

If you are shopping for casseroles—I have quite a variety but always need more—be sure to match your other serving pieces, as well as dining room or terrace décor. Casseroles are designed in many fascinating styles and colors. You will find elegant classical shapes that are perfect for formal tables, gay pieces that catch the spirit of peasant pottery, and simple pieces to go with modern tableware.

Casseroles are made of many materials too. Enameled cast-iron is flameproof and ovenproof, and can be used on top of the stove, in the oven, or under the broiler. Glazed stoneware or ceramic ware distributes heat more slowly and evenly, but can be used on top of the stove only over an asbestos mat. You can buy casseroles at all prices, from inexpensive glass ones sold with handsome trivets to luxurious copper or stainless steel ones.

If you can be specialized in your casserole shopping, look for big Mexican pottery pieces for serving arroz con pollo, tamale pie, or other dishes of similar origin. Shallow oval casseroles fit the shape of fish, so use them for baking the sea's produce. Match your other appointments too. Big wooden bread baskets, woven trays, and colorful rough-textured clothes and coffee mugs are appropriate for an informal table. Stainless steel is smoothly perfect for more formal tables, and you will find enameled cast iron that is an excellent match for some patterns of fine dinner china.

what size casserole?

Many sizes are available. If possible, have casseroles with varying capacities, and also matched individual ones that hold a cup to a pint. When not in the oven, use them on your buffet table to hold curry condiments or relishes, soups or salads. The most popular of all sizes is one which holds 1½ quarts, but two-quart casseroles run a very close second. My largest casserole (which I sometimes use as a salad bowl) has a capacity of five quarts—which is none too generous when I entertain four sisters, one brother, and assorted in-laws, nieces, and nephews, all at one time as I do.

Since many casseroles (particularly imported ones) are manufactured in odd sizes, I have sometimes suggested "small," "medium," or "large," rather than given a specific size. For small, any casserole with a capacity of less than 1½ quarts may be used. For medium, 1½ to 2-quart capacity is ideal. For large, use any casserole with a capacity greater than 2½ quarts. If you do not have casseroles of the recommended size, divide the recipe to fit available containers.

hints for buffet parties

Buffet parties make it easier for you to entertain large crowds without a maid, and with little table space. Here are some suggestions for buffets:

1. Do be sure to make your table exciting and interesting. Match your food, theme, colors, and the spirit of your hospitality. If your mood is formal, nothing but your most elegant and delicate ware will do. And a champagne casserole or the like belongs with such a meal.

Do be sure to try unusual decorations. An inexpensive fish net makes a fine cloth for parties with a nautical theme. For Hawaiian parties, use a fruit arrangement of bananas, coconuts, avocados, pineapples, and lots of green leaves. Make paper leis by sewing together artificial or real flowers. If your accent is Italian, a gay checked cloth, wine bottles in woven reed baskets, Italian pottery figures, and a travel poster in the background would make an interesting table. Even your music should belong to the theme—so check your record collection as well as your pantry before your next party.

2. Plant a fruit, vegetable or flower arrangement as a focal point. Many books show beginners how to make handsome designs. An excellent one, FRUIT AND VEGETABLE ARRANGEMENTS by Emma H. Cyphers is published by Hearthside Press. It gives directions for more than 100 arrangements for the table, many using inexpensive plant materials. One of the most unusual features ordinary garden cucumbers and foliage to make a dramatically modern arrangement.

3. If foods go from oven to table for immediate service, they will stay piping hot enroute and retain heat and flavor throughout the meal. But if there are delays in service and late comers, candle warmers to put under casseroles are a worthwhile investment. Trivets or trays under casseroles protect your table tops.

4. If casseroles must wait in the oven, be sure there is enough liquid to keep them from drying out. Turn oven heat down to 200°, and add small quantities of hot water, sauce, or stock as needed.

5. Be sure salad is crisp. Use at least two kinds of lettuce. Wash them the morning of the party or the day before. Dry. Wrap in a tea towel and store in refrigerator until ready to use.

6. Add vegetables with lots of moisture, such as tomatoes, at last minute. Otherwise they will wilt greens.

7. Add dressing just a few minutes before salad will be served. Be sure all leaves are thoroughly coated. Use an excellent dressing such as the following:

my favorite French Dressing

Make a quart of this dressing at a time and store in a cool place. It will keep for months and improves as it stands.

Put ¾ cup of good tarragon or basil vinegar into a quart bottle or Mason jar. With needle, string a garlic clove on long white thread. Drop garlic into vinegar so that the ends of thread dangle outside jar. Add 2 tablespoons salt, 1 tablespoon dry mustard, ½ tablespoon pepper. Cover jar and let stand for several days, shaking frequently. After a few days, discard garlic and fill the jar with good olive or salad oil. You will need almost 3 cups of oil. Shake well. Add more salt and vinegar if you like a sharp taste. Toss greens in large bowl so all leaves get the dressing. Vary French dressing by adding to taste: Worcestershire, chili or tabasco sauce, herbs and spices of all kinds.

a basic medium white sauce

If you do not have your own recipe for white sauce, here is a standard one which makes I cup:
Melt 2 tablespoons butter over very low heat. Stir in 2 tablespoons flour. Keep stirring until smooth. Slowly add 1 cup milk, ¾ teaspoon salt, and a dash of pepper. Cook 10-15 minutes at very low heat until smooth and thick.

Vary sauce by changing the liquid. Use leftover vegetable chicken or beef stock, substitute light cream for milk, and add seasonings such as Worcestershire, curry powder, onion juice, paprika and the like to make pleasant changes in the basic recipe. Just be sure to taste as you add. If sauce becomes too thick, thin with more liquid.

how to freeze casseroles

1. Undercook vegetables and macaroni that are to be heated after freezing, as they will finish cooking when they are reheated.

2. Add crumb and cheese toppings to casseroles after freezing, when casserole is ready to be baked for serving.

3. Cool cooked food quickly by surrounding pan with ice water. Transfer to freezer container.

4. Select a container that is just right for one meal for your company or family, or freeze in one-portion containers. Use rigid aluminum-foil containers with their own tight covers, or freeze right in the casserole in which food was baked.

5. Label casseroles, seal packages tightly to eliminate air and retain moisture.

6. Do not thaw casseroles which are fully cooked. Put them into oven in ovenproof casserole and bake at 400° for maximum time given in the recipe.

7. If you must transfer frozen food to casserole for heating, thaw package in warm water just long enough to make transfer easier.

8. To bake food which has been partially cooked, as for instance chicken which has been browned in saucepan but is not yet tender, bake in oven at temperature given in recipe, but add half an hour to the time.

9. If you cannot spare a casserole for freezer, line casserole with aluminum foil. Add cooled food, either partly or wholly cooked. Freeze. As soon as frozen, remove foil and continue to store in freezer. When ready to serve, put frozen foil package back in casserole and follow preceding directions for heating.

10. For maximum flavor, cooked casseroles stored at zero temperature or lower should be used within three months of freezing.

DELICIOUS EGG, CHEESE AND PASTA COMBINATIONS

Eggs Bombay : Sunday Supper Casserole : Eggplant Parmigiana : Casserole of Cheese Pancakes : Strata : Blue Cheese Casserole : Lasagne Bolognese : Nancy's Lasagne : California Burgundy Supper : Kasha Casserole : Spaghetti and Eggplant : Noodle, Cheese and Vegetable Casserole : Arroz y Queso Mexicano : Casserole of Savory Spanish Rice : Rice Pepper and Pineapple Casserole : Riso Neapolitan

Eggs Bombay

OVEN TIME: 20-30 MINUTES AT 350°   4 SERVINGS

5 tablespoons butter
1 cup sliced onions
2 teaspoons curry powder
4 hard-cooked eggs
4 tomatoes, cut into thick slices
Salt and pepper
3 tablespoons grated Parmesan cheese
1 cup medium cream sauce
2 cups cooked rice
¼ cup cream

Melt butter and cook onions until soft. Stir in curry powder. Push onions to side. Cut eggs into thick slices and brown them in center of pan with onions. Arrange tomato slices in greased individual casseroles. Sprinkle with salt, pepper and grated cheese. Top with sautéed egg slices and onions. Now spoon on cream sauce. Add equal portions of rice to each casserole and moisten with cream. Cover and bake in moderate oven until steaming hot. If casseroles do not have covers, use aluminum foil. For a late Sunday morning breakfast.

brunch with a foreign accent

CHICKEN LIVER AND BACON KEBABS. Cut 4 chicken livers and bacon slices in half. Wrap bacon around liver. Fasten with toothpick. Bake on shallow pan same time and temperature as eggs until done.

EGGS BOMBAY   CHILLED CANTALOUPE RINGS. Peel cantaloupe. Cut in rings, remove seeds, fill centers with preserved sliced kumquats, chutney, or green seeded grapes. HOT BISCUITS   COFFEE

Sunday Supper Casserole

OVEN TIME: 20 MINUTES AT 350°   4-6 SERVINGS

6 hard-cooked eggs
3 peeled tomatoes, not too ripe
4 tablespoons butter
4 tablespoons flour
1½ cups milk
2 teaspoons salt
½ cup grated cheese
2 tablespoons shredded pimentos
¼ cup buttered fine cracker crumbs

Cut eggs into halves and arrange them as a border in a buttered medium casserole. Peel tomatoes by spearing with a fork and holding over flame until skin blisters. Cut them into thick slices and pile in center of casserole. Make sauce on top of stove: Melt butter, blend in flour, slowly stir in milk, and salt. Cook for a few minutes over low flame until sauce begins to thicken. Remove from heat, add cheese and let it melt. Pour into casserole, top with pimentos and crumbs. Bake 20 minutes. For a complete supper, serve with cooked rice.

open house

SUNDAY SUPPER CASSEROLE   PARSLEY RICE. Cook 1 cup rice. Add butter and chopped parsley.

FRUIT SALAD. On individual plates, arrange groups of peeled orange and grapefruit sections, a bunch of seeded green grapes, 2 banana chunks rolled in chopped nuts, red cherries or strawberries on stems, peach halves, canned pineapple ring, a mound of cottage cheese.

FRUIT DRESSING. Shake ¼ cup orange juice, 1 teaspoon lemon juice, 2 tablespoons salad oil, 1 teaspoon sugar, ¾ teaspoon salt.

CHEESE BISCUITS. Serve them hot, wrapped in napkin.

Eggplant Parmigiana

OVEN TIME: 15-20 MINUTES AT 375°   4 SERVINGS

1 medium eggplant, cut into slices ¼ inch thick
3 tablespoons olive oil
6 ripe tomatoes, chopped
2 tablespoons tomato paste
Salt and pepper
2 cups coarse bread crumbs
½ cup grated Parmesan cheese
1 tablespoon chopped parsley
2 cloves garlic, finely crushed
8 thin slices mozzarella cheese

Cover eggplant slices with salted water and let stand ½ hour. Drain and dry. Sauté them in hot oil in large skillet until soft and lightly brown on both sides. Transfer to platter. In same skillet, combine tomatoes, tomato paste, salt and pepper, and let simmer for at least half an hour. Mix together bread crumbs, Parmesan cheese, parsley, and garlic. Arrange a layer of browned eggplant slices in greased casserole, sprinkle with bread crumb mixture and pour in some tomato sauce. Repeat layers until everything is used. End with a layer of eggplant slices. Top with mozzarella cheese. Bake until cheese browns.

on a Saturday night

HAMBURGERS EN BROCHETTE. To ½ pound chopped prime beef add ½ teaspoon salt, dash pepper, 2 teaspoons lemon juice. Mix. Shape into patties 1-inch in diameter. Bake in shallow pan same time as eggplant. Serve on toothpicks.

EGGPLANT PARMIGIANA   SALAD. Sliced tomatoes and anchovy fillets with lemon juice and anchovy oil. ITALIAN BREADSTICKS

Casserole of Cheese Pancakes

OVEN TIME: 10-15 MINUTES AT 350°   4-5 SERVINGS

2¼ cups milk
2 cups pancake mix
1 pound pork sausage links, cooked
15 slices American cheese

Add milk to pancake flour. Mix and stir *lightly* as slightly lumpy batter makes fluffy pancakes. Using a ¼ cup measure, pour batter for each pancake onto a hot lightly greased griddle. Bake to a golden brown, turning once. Make stacks of three pancakes each with a slice of cheese between each one. Top each stack with 2 sausage links and a slice of cheese. Place in 5 shallow individual casseroles and bake in oven until cheese is melted. Serve immediately. With pancake flour on your shelves —or the mixings to make your own—you are equipped to handle unexpected guests in fine style.

supper for friends who drop in

(A pleasant snack for expected company too. You can cook the sausages at the table in one of the new electric skillets, bake the pancakes in the skillet too, then whisk the casserole off to the oven to be finished.)

CASSEROLE OF CHEESE PANCAKES   SPICY GLAZED APPLES. Combine in saucepan ½ cup sugar, ½ cup water, 1 tablespoon vinegar. Cook slowly until sugar dissolves. Stir in 4 sticks cinnamon and 2 cloves. Cut 2 cored apples crosswise in half. Put into baking dish, cover with sirup and bake in oven same time as pancakes. Serve together.   HOT COFFEE

Strata

OVEN TIME: 25 MINUTES AT 325°   4 SERVINGS

6 slices bread
Softened butter
1½ cups cubed aged cheddar cheese
½ teaspoon salt
⅛ teaspoon pepper
2 eggs, slightly beaten
2 cups milk

Spread bread with softened butter. Cut slices into inch squares. Transfer to greased small casserole. Top with cheese cubes. Season with salt and pepper. Combine eggs and milk. Pour into casserole. Bake until cheese melts and custard sets. Full of good nourishment and pleasing flavor.

Sunday brunch

MINTED MELON AND GRAPES. Cut melon with potato ball cutter. Refrigerate. Just before serving in individual plates, combine with ½ cup seedless grapes. Sprinkle ¼ cup orange juice over fruit. Garnish with mint leaves. STRATA   BAKED BACON. Place 12 strips of bacon, not overlapping, on rack in shallow baking pan. Put on top shelf of oven, bake same time as strata, or until done. No turning or draining is necessary.

CURRIED BROILED TOMATOES. Cut 4 unpeeled medium tomatoes crosswise in halves. Brush with 2 tablespoons melted butter, a dash of curry powder, salt and pepper. Broil 6-8 minutes until light brown.

HOT COFFEE

Blue Cheese Casserole

OVEN TIME: 20 MINUTES AT 350°   4-6 SERVINGS

4 cups seasoned mashed potatoes
1 cup blue cheese
1 cup walnut meats, chopped
1 large onion, finely minced
1 teaspoon salt
½ teaspoon pepper
½ tablespoon melted butter

Grease a medium casserole with butter. Line bottom with half
of the mashed potatoes. Combine cheese, nuts, onion, salt and
pepper. Mix well. Spread over potatoes in casserole. Top with
remainder of mashed potatoes. Smooth potatoes evenly out to
edges. Sprinkle melted butter over top. Bake in moderate oven
until done. This is worth trying, though the combination seems
odd.

six for supper

BLUE CHEESE CASSEROLE   APPLE, ORANGE AND ONION SALAD. Peel and
slice 2 large oranges, 1 Bermuda onion, 2 large eating apples.
Remove cores from apples. Sprinkle with lemon juice to pre-
vent discoloring. Cut large green pepper into thin slices. Seed.
On individual salad plates arrange overlapping slices of orange,
onion, apple, green pepper. Sprinkle with minced scallions.
Serve chilled with French dressing.   CRISP TOASTED ROLLS.
Heat in oven.

NUT CAKE   COFFEE

Lasagne Bolognese

OVEN TIME: 20 MINUTES AT 375°   4-6 SERVINGS

½ pound lasagne
1 tablespoon olive oil
½ pound ground beef
½ stalk celery, finely chopped
½ onion, chopped
½ teaspoon parsley
½ clove garlic
1 No. 2½ can tomatoes
1 can tomato paste
¼ teaspoon salt
Dash of pepper
Dash of nutmeg
Dash of orégano
½ pound mozzarella cheese, thinly sliced
2 tablespoons grated Parmesan cheese

Cook lasagne in boiling salted water until almost tender. Drain and rinse. In saucepan, heat oil and brown beef, celery, onion, parsley and garlic. When beef is no longer red, add tomatoes, tomato paste, salt, pepper, nutmeg and orégano. Let simmer 1½ hours to make a thick sauce. In greased large casserole, arrange alternate layers of cooked lasagne, meat sauce and mozzarella, ending with sauce. Sprinkle with Parmesan cheese. Bake until cheese is melted. Serve very hot. A generous helping of lasagne, a mixed salad and fruit for dessert—a perfect dinner.

bridge luncheon

LASAGNE BOLOGNESE   WATERCRESS SALAD
RASPBERRY SHERBET   COFFEE

Nancy's Lasagne

OVEN TIME: 20 MINUTES AT 350°   6-8 SERVINGS

1 pound pork shoulder, cut into small pieces
1 tablespoon olive oil
½ onion, minced
1 clove garlic, minced
1 teaspoon minced parsley
Salt and pepper
1½ small cans tomato paste
2 cups warm water
1 pound lasagne
1 pound ricotta (Italian pot cheese)
4 tablespoons grated Parmesan cheese

Place pork in saucepan with oil, onion, garlic and parsley and brown thoroughly on all sides. Remove pork and keep warm. To saucepan, add salt, pepper and tomato paste diluted in 2 cups warm water. Cover and cook 2 hours, adding a little water from time to time if necessary. This should make about 2 cups of tomato sauce. In large pot of boiling salted water cook lasagne until tender, stirring frequently to keep them from sticking together. Drain. Mix ricotta with 1 tablespoon warm water to make soft paste. In a greased large casserole arrange lasagne in layers, alternating with pork, sauce, ricotta and Parmesan, until lasagne is all used. End with a layer each of sauce, ricotta and Parmesan. Bake until done and serve hot.

provincial party

Pot plants of geraniums or African violets on harmonizing cloth would make fine centerpiece.

NANCY'S LASAGNE   MIXED GREEN SALAD   ITALIAN VINO   HOT
FRENCH OR ITALIAN BREAD   WATERMELON CHUNKS

California Burgundy Supper

OVEN TIME: 1 HOUR AT 350°   SERVES 6

6 slices bacon, chopped
1 large onion, chopped
1 green pepper, chopped
1 can condensed tomato soup
½ cup Burgundy wine
1 4-ounce can mushrooms, undrained
2 cups cream-style corn
½ pound (2 cups) grated American cheese
Salt and pepper
½ pound spaghetti, cooked and drained

Fry bacon, onion and green pepper together until bacon is done and onion and pepper are soft. Stir frequently. Add tomato soup, wine, mushrooms, corn, 1 cup cheese, salt and pepper, and spaghetti. Mix well. Turn into medium casserole, sprinkle with remainder of cheese and bake in oven until done. Serve from casserole. Wine, cheese and spaghetti are perfect go-togethers.

California supper

(Makes a substantial luncheon too)

CALIFORNIA BURGUNDY SUPPER   CRUSTY FRENCH BREAD WITH GARLIC BUTTER. Buy loaf, cut slices almost through to bottom. Spread slices on both sides with garlic butter (finely chopped or pounded garlic cloves blended with butter). Heat in oven 10 minutes. Serve warm.

BURGUNDY WINE. Rest of bottle.   FRESH FRUIT BOWL   BEVERAGE

Kasha Casserole

OVEN TIME: 20-30 MINUTES AT 350°   4 SERVINGS

5 tablespoons butter
1 cup sliced mushrooms
1½ cups coarse buckwheat groats
⅓ cup finely chopped onions
Salt and pepper
4 cups chicken consommé

Heat 2 tablespoons butter in skillet and gently brown mushrooms, stirring them frequently. Transfer to buttered medium casserole. Add 3 tablespoons butter to skillet. Put in groats and sauté over low flame for 10 minutes. Add onions, salt, pepper and chicken consommé. Cover and cook for 20 minutes, stirring frequently. If kasha becomes dry, add boiling water or consommé. Turn into casserole containing mushrooms and mix gently with a fork. Cover and bake until kasha is fluffy but still moist.

buffet à la russe

APPETIZER TRAY. Black caviar, slices of salt herring, mound of chopped onion, sliced cucumbers, radish roses, thin slices black bread.

CHILLED VODKA   THIN SLICES COOKED CHICKEN AND HAM

KASHA CASSEROLE   CHEESE BLINI. Buy delicious frozen ones. Serve piping hot as dessert with cold commercially-made sour cream.

BEVERAGE

Spaghetti and Eggplant

OVEN TIME: 30 MINUTES AT 375°   8 SERVINGS

12 ounces spaghetti
1 eggplant
Salt and pepper
½ cup flour
¼ cup olive oil
1 medium onion, chopped
1 clove garlic
1 No. 2 can tomatoes
¼ cup cubed American cheese

Cook spaghetti in lots of boiling salted water until tender but do not overcook it. Drain and wash with cold water. Pare eggplant and cut into slices ¼ inch thick. Sprinkle with salt, pepper and flour. Heat oil in large skillet and brown eggplant slices lightly on both sides. Transfer half the slices to a greased medium casserole and cover with the drained spaghetti. Brown onion and garlic in skillet. Add tomatoes, bring to boil and transfer to casserole. Add remaining eggplant slices and sprinkle with cheese. Cover and bake until cheese melts.

summer supper

SPAGHETTI AND EGGPLANT   SUMMER SALAD. Arrange chunks of tomatoes, cucumbers, scallions, lettuce and radishes on shredded lettuce in individual bowls. Dress with commercial sour cream.
MELBA TOAST ROUNDS WITH PARSLEY BUTTER. With a fork, blend 2 tablespoons chopped parsley with ¼ cup butter.

Noodle, Cheese and Vegetable Casserole

OVEN TIME: 30 MINUTES AT 350°   6 SERVINGS

¾ pound noodles
1 cup creamed cottage cheese
6 ounces cream cheese
1½ cups commercial sour cream
1 cup cooked vegetables, drained
1 teaspoon salt
¼ teaspoon pepper
⅓ cup chopped scallions or chives
Butter

Cook noodles in boiling salted water until tender. Drain and keep warm. Blend together cottage cheese, cream cheese and 1 cup of sour cream. Reserve remainder of cream for topping. Fold cheese mixture into noodles; add cooked vegetables, and season with salt and pepper. Toss gently with a fork until well mixed. Sprinkle with chopped scallions or chives. Cover with remaining sour cream, dot with butter, and bake until bubbling and very hot. You can't go wrong with this for luncheon.

luncheon for six

NOODLE, CHEESE AND VEGETABLE CASSEROLE   SANDWICH PLATTER.
Make sandwiches of thin slices of buttered whole wheat bread and sliced cucumbers; buttered white bread spread with devilled ham.

PEPPERMINT ICE CREAM   BEVERAGE

Arroz y Queso Mexicano

OVEN TIME: 15-20 MINUTES AT 350°   8 SERVINGS

¼ cup fat or drippings
¾ cup chopped onions
¼ cup chopped minced celery
¼ cup chopped green pepper
1¼ cups uncooked rice (the kind that doesn't need washing)
2½ cups tomatoes
1 teaspoon salt
¼ teaspoon pepper
½ teaspoon chili powder
2 bouillon cubes
1½ cups grated or cubed American cheese
⅔ cup chopped cooked ham

Heat fat in saucepan. Cook onions, celery and green pepper until soft but not brown. Remove. Brown rice lightly. Combine with onions, celery and pepper. Turn into greased large casserole. In same saucepan, combine tomatoes, bouillon cubes, salt, pepper and chili powder. Bring to quick boil. Be sure that cubes are dissolved. Turn into casserole. Sprinkle with cheese and ham. Bake, uncovered, until rice is grainy and tender, but not mushy. This Mexican rice and cheese meal will do you proud as a company luncheon or supper.

fiesta time

ARROZ Y QUESO MEXICANO   HOT ROLLS OR TAMALES   STRING BEAN SALAD. Cook 2 pounds string beans until tender. Chill. Sprinkle with ½ cup oil, 2 tablespoons vinegar, finely chopped onion, salt and pepper.

CARAMEL CUSTARD. Follow recipe in basic cookbook, bake in square loaf pan set in pan of water. Just before serving, pour 6 tablespoons heated brandy (cold won't blaze) over pudding. Set aflame.   BEVERAGE

Casserole of Savory Spanish Rice

OVEN TIME: 35 MINUTES AT 350°   4 SERVINGS

8 small sausages
1 clove garlic, mashed
3 tablespoons olive oil
1 large sweet onion, chopped
1 green pepper, chopped
2 large tomatoes, chopped
1 cup uncooked rice
2 tablespoons chopped parsley
1 cup beef stock, or bouillon cube dissolved in hot water
Salt and pepper to taste
Pinch of saffron

Brown sausages and garlic in hot oil for 2 minutes. Add onion, green pepper and tomatoes, and sauté 3 more minutes. Add rice and parsley and sauté until rice is golden brown. Pour in beef stock. Sprinkle with salt, pepper and saffron. Transfer to casserole and bake until done. If you have left-over cooked chopped giblets, they can be added to this casserole. Sauté them with the sausages.

Spanish style party supper

APPETIZER TRAY. Olives, devilled eggs, olives, cold cuts, olives.

SHERRY WINE   CASSEROLE OF SAVORY SPANISH RICE

STUFFED PIMENTO SALAD. Cream with fork 3 ounces cream cheese, 2 tablespoons cream, ½ cup chopped olives, salt and pepper. Carefully stuff 6 canned pimentos with mixture. Chill. Slice crosswise. Serve on shredded lettuce with French dressing.

ORANGE SHERBET   COFFEE

Rice, Pepper and Pineapple Casserole

OVEN TIME: 40-45 MINUTES AT 350°   6 SERVINGS

3 tablespoons oil or butter
1 cup raw rice
1 green pepper, minced
2 cups canned pineapple chunks
Butter
2 cups chicken stock (or 2 bouillon cubes dissolved in
    boiling water)
4 tablespoons pineapple sirup

In a large skillet, heat oil. Add rice and let it cook until golden, stirring frequently so it does not become too brown. Remove rice. Now cook green pepper until it is soft. Remove. Add some more oil or butter and fry pineapple chunks until brown. In a well-greased casserole arrange a layer of golden rice, a layer of green pepper, and a layer of pineapple. Dot with butter. Repeat layers until all the rice, pepper and pineapple are used. Heat chicken stock and pineapple sirup in skillet. Stir so that all sediment is loosened from the pan. As soon as it boils, pour into casserole. Cover and bake in moderate oven until rice is tender.

buffet after bridge

(For a company supper, add bowls of cream of mushroom or chicken soup, serve in petite marmites or small casseroles.)

SLICED CHICKEN ON BUTTERED BAKING POWDER BISCUITS

RICE, PEPPER AND PINEAPPLE CASSEROLE

BUTTER PECAN ICE CREAM   COOKIES   COFFEE

Riso Neapolitan

OVEN TIME: 20-30 MINUTES AT 375°   6 SERVINGS

½ pound chopped beefsteak
1 egg, slightly beaten
½ teaspoon grated lemon rind
½ cup soft bread crumbs
½ teaspoon salt
Dash of pepper
3 tablespoons olive oil
½ cup buttered fine crumbs
4 cups cooked rice
1 cup mozzarella or Bel Paese cheese, cut up
¼ cup chopped chicken or turkey giblets, or minced
    prosciutto
1 cup cooked green peas
1½ cups tomato sauce

1. Combine chopped beef, egg, lemon rind, soft bread crumbs, salt and pepper. Shape mixture into 12 or more tiny balls. Fry in hot oil, turning to brown them all over.
2. In well greased casserole, spread half the buttered fine crumbs. Lay half the rice over crumbs.
3. Now, using half of each food, spoon in layers of browned beef balls, mozzarella or Bel Paese cheese, giblets, peas, and tomato sauce. Repeat layers. Top with grated Parmesan cheese and remainder of buttered crumbs. Bake in moderate oven without a cover until top is crusty.

on a winter evening

RISO NEAPOLITAN   GREEN PEPPER SALAD. Hold 6 green peppers over flame until skin blisters. Peel. Cut in strips, arrange in flat serving dish, refrigerate 1 hour in French dressing.
BRANDIED PEACHES   COFFEE

FABULOUS FISH AND SHELLFISH CASSEROLES

Fillets of Striped Bass Bonne Femme : Montauk Bake : Flounder and Eggplant Parmigiana : Savory Halibut and Broccoli Casserole : Fluffy Salmon Soufflées : Sole en Papillotes : New Orleans Trout in Sea Food Sauce : Arroz Con Mariscos : Scallops Baked in Garlic Sauce : Sheepshead Bay Casserole : Old Charleston Shrimp and Corn Casserole : Baked Tuna with Brazil Nuts : Tuna Party Casserole

Fillets of Striped Bass Bonne Femme

OVEN TIME: 15-20 MINUTES AT 350°   4 SERVINGS

2 pounds bass fillets (save bone)
3 peppercorns
1 clove garlic
2 slices onion
1 cup water
½ cup white wine
1 teaspoon chopped shallots or chives
1 teaspoon chopped parsley
Salt and pepper
1 cup sliced mushrooms
3 egg yolks
3 tablespoons butter

1. Put fish bones in saucepan with peppercorns, garlic, onion, water, and wine. Bring to boil, then simmer for half an hour to make fish stock. Strain and reserve.
2. Sprinkle a buttered medium casserole with shallots and parsley. Place fish in pan. Season with salt and pepper and top with sliced mushrooms. Pour in fish stock.
3. Bake in moderate oven until fish is done, about 10 minutes.
4. Remove fish to hot serving platter. Thicken sauce in casserole by adding egg yolks and butter. Serve very hot over fish.

supper on the special side

FILLETS OF STRIPED BASS BONNE FEMME   POTATO PUFFS. Heat frozen ones same time as fish.   SPINACH PARMESAN. Use 2 cups chopped cooked spinach. Drain; save liquid. Make 1 cup white sauce using spinach liquid for part of milk. Remove from heat, add 2 ounces grated Parmesan cheese. Put over spinach in casserole, cover with crumbs, bake 10 minutes. Sauce may be made ahead and reheated at table in chafing dish.

STRAWBERRIES MARINATED IN KIRSCH LIQUEUR   BEVERAGE

Montauk Bake

OVEN TIME: 20-25 MINUTES AT 375°   4-6 SERVINGS

1 pound fish fillets, fresh or frozen and thawed
3 tablespoons butter
¼ cup chopped onion
¼ cup chopped green pepper
3 tablespoons shredded pimentos
1 can condensed celery soup, undiluted
1 cup cooked or canned shrimp
¼ cup sliced mushrooms
Salt and pepper
2 cups seasoned mashed potatoes
Butter

Cut fillets into ¾-inch cubes. Melt butter in saucepan. Cook onion, peppers and pimentos until soft. Stir in soup, shrimp, fish and half the mushrooms (save the other half for garnishing). Season with salt and pepper. Gently spoon mixture into greased medium casserole. Line sides with potatoes and brush with butter. Garnish center with remainder of mushrooms. Bake until fish is tender. Do not overcook . . . timing is your clue to moist well-flavored fish.

shore dinner

MONTAUK BAKE   TOMATO JELLY SALAD RING. Put through grinder 2 cups tomatoes, 1 cup celery, ½ small onion. Add 2 teaspoons lemon juice, ½ teaspoon salt, dash vinegar. Dissolve 1 envelope gelatin in few tablespoons cold water. Add ¾ cup boiling water. Combine with ground vegetables. Pour into 4-6 greased custard cups. Chill 4 hours. Unmold on individual plates.   PARSLEY BISCUITS   HOT BLUEBERRY PIE   COFFEE

Flounder and Eggplant Parmigiana

OVEN TIME: 30 MINUTES AT 325°   6 SERVINGS

1 eggplant, sliced
2 cloves garlic, finely minced or crushed
¼ cup oil
1 cup tomato sauce
Salt and pepper
Dash of oregano
1½ pounds flounder fillets
¼ cup grated Parmesan cheese
3 tablespoons butter

Soak eggplant in salted water for 15 minutes. Drain and dry. Sauté slices in hot oil with garlic. Discard garlic and transfer eggplant to buttered shallow casserole. Spoon ½ cup tomato sauce over eggplant. Season with salt, pepper and oregano. Place flounder fillets on top of sauce. Add the remaining sauce, sprinkle with cheese, and dot with butter. Cover casserole and bake until fish is done.

lunching with an Italian accent

FLOUNDER AND EGGPLANT PARMIGIANA   PORCUPINE PEACH AND CREAM CHEESE SALAD. Cream together 3 ounces cream cheese, 2 tablespoons fresh cream, 2 tablespoons finely chopped chives or scallions. Fill hollows of 3 large halved peaches with mixture. Turn filled side down onto bed of shredded lettuce in individual salad plates. Cut toasted almonds lengthwise into thin strips. Insert into peaches as quills. Decorate edge of plate with ring of green pepper.

HOT ITALIAN OR FRENCH BREAD   FRUIT   COFFEE

Savory Halibut and Broccoli Casserole

OVEN TIME: 40-50 MINUTES AT 375°   4 SERVINGS

4 halibut steaks, about 2 pounds
2 tablespoons lemon juice
½ pound salt pork (about 8 thin slices)
½ cup thinly-sliced onions
2 pounds broccoli, cooked and drained (cut off tough
    stems before cooking)
1 bay leaf, crumpled
3 tablespoons butter or margarine
3 tablespoons flour
¾ cup crushed cracker crumbs
1 tablespoon paprika

Brush halibut steaks with lemon juice. Mince all but two slices
of salt pork and sprinkle into greased shallow casserole. Top
with onion and broccoli. Add bits of bay leaf. Now place halibut steaks in casserole. Blend butter and flour, and spread over
fish. Add crumbs mixed with paprika. Lay thin slices of pork
on top. Bake in moderate oven until fish is done.

Lenten luncheon

SAVORY HALIBUT AND BROCCOLI CASSEROLE   CARROT BAKE. Cut 1½
    pounds young carrots into thin slices, arrange in baking dish,
    barely cover with boiling water. Sprinkle with salt and melted
    butter. Cover and bake until tender. Same time as halibut.
    Serve with chopped parsley.   HOT CORN BREAD   BEVERAGE

Fluffy Salmon Soufflées

OVEN TIME: 10 MINUTES AT 450°   4-6 SERVINGS

1½ cups flaked drained salmon
2 cups seasoned mashed potatoes
2 eggs, slightly beaten
½ teaspoon celery salt
Dash of pepper
3 tablespoons buttered bread crumbs

Combine all ingredients except bread crumbs. Pat on lightly floured board. Cut into squares. Roll in buttered crumbs. Place in greased shallow casserole and bake in preheated oven until very brown and hot.

Do not bake soufflées for more than ten minutes. If baked too long, they will dry. May be served with hollandaise sauce poured over each square.

light supper tonight

CHILLED VICHYSOISSE OR TOMATO JUICE WITH CUCUMBER SLICES

FLUFFY SALMON SOUFFLÉES   SPRING SALAD. Combine 1 cup each of crisp sliced cucumbers, radishes, and watercress. Just before serving, toss with ¾ cup French dressing. Serve on romaine lettuce.

TRAY OF ASSORTED BREADS AND CHEESES   FRESH FRUIT   COFFEE

Sole en Papillotes

OVEN TIME: 20-25 MINUTES AT 400°   6 SERVINGS

2 tablespoons butter
2 cups flaked crab meat
2 small onions, finely chopped
1 cup mushrooms, chopped
2 tablespoons flour
1½ cups fish stock (boil 2 cups salted water with fish heads,
    fins, tails, bones, and onion)
1 tablespoon chopped mixed fresh herbs
2 egg yolks
¾ teaspoon salt
¼ teaspoon pepper
3 tablespoons sherry wine
6 sole (or flounder) fillets, 2½ pounds

1. Melt half the butter. Lightly brown crab meat. Remove from pan and reserve for later use.
2. Add remainder of butter to pan and slowly cook onions and mushrooms. Stir in flour and fish stock. Simmer for 10 minutes. Remove from heat. Add herbs, egg yolks, salt and pepper. Simmer again at very low heat for about 5 minutes until sauce begins to thicken. Remove from heat and stir in wine.
3. Put fillets on flat surface and spread them with browned crab and enough sauce to moisten. Roll up as for jelly roll. Secure with toothpicks or string.
4. Arrange each fish roll on one end of greased parchment paper 8x5 inches. Top with more sauce. Fold free ends of paper over fillets, and close edges. Bake on shallow pan in hot oven. Cut crosswise slits in paper and serve hot from oven.

New Orleans Trout in Sea Food Sauce

OVEN TIME: 20-25 MINUTES AT 375°   6-8 SERVINGS

3 pounds trout, cut into fillets
3 tablespoons butter
3 tablespoons olive oil
1 small onion, finely chopped
1 garlic clove, finely minced or crushed
½ pound mushrooms, sliced
1 teaspoon powdered thyme and rosemary (optional but
    better if used)
1 teaspoon chopped parsley
1½ cups sherry wine
12 shucked oysters
½ pound fresh shrimp, shelled and veined
Salt and pepper

Place the trout fillets into a greased shallow casserole. Make
sauce in saucepan: Melt butter, add oil, onion, garlic and mushrooms and cook until soft but not brown. Stir in powdered
herbs and parsley, then slowly mix in wine, oysters and shrimp.
Season to taste with salt and pepper. Blend well. Cook over
low heat for a few minutes. Now pour over trout and bake until
done.

creole luncheon

NEW ORLEANS TROUT IN SEA FOOD SAUCE   GREEN SALAD BOWL. Rub
wooden salad bowl with cut garlic clove. Break 1 head crisp
romaine lettuce and 1 heart of chicory into bowl. Combine ¼
cup salad oil, 1 tablespoon vinegar, ½ teaspoon salt, ½ teaspoon
paprika, ⅛ teaspoon dry mustard. Sprinkle over greens and toss
thoroughly.   HOT CURRIED BISCUITS   COFFEE

Arroz Con Mariscos

OVEN TIME: 30-40 MINUTES AT 350°   8 SERVINGS

1 cup celery slices
½ cup chopped pimentos
¼ cup chopped onion
3 cloves garlic, finely minced or crushed
¼ cup olive oil
3 cups chicken stock or water
2 cups raw rice
1½ cups cooked crab meat, flaked
1 pound peeled raw shrimp
3 tablespoons tomato paste
2 teaspoon salt
½ teaspoon pepper (cayenne for a hot taste)
Few threads Spanish saffron

Cook celery, pimentos, onion and garlic in a large skillet in hot oil until soft. Add chicken stock or water and as soon as mixture boils, add other ingredients. Bring to boil again. Taste for seasoning. Put into a large greased casserole (or 2 small ones) cover tightly and bake in medium oven until done. A superb Spanish rice and seafood casserole.

super Spanish supper

ARROZ CON MARISCOS   AVOCADO AND GREEN GRAPES SALAD. Peel 4 avocados, cut in half lengthwise. Remove stones. Sprinkle halves with lemon juice. Combine ½ cup each cut-up lettuce and watercress. Add 1 cup canned drained peas. Combine ½ cup French dressing with ⅓ cup bottled chili sauce, 1 teaspoon grated onion. Serve over salad.
HOT CRISP BISCUITS   SHERRY

Scallops Baked in Garlic Sauce

OVEN TIME: 10-22 MINUTES AT 350°   6 SERVINGS

2 pounds bay scallops (or sea scallops cut in half)
3 gloves garlic, covered with boiling water
1 cup butter
½ cup sliced mushrooms
¼ teaspoon salt
⅛ teaspoon pepper
¼ cup fine bread crumbs

Wipe scallops. Drain garlic cloves, and mash or pound them in butter until well blended. Lightly grease a small casserole with part of the garlic butter. Put in mushrooms. Arrange scallops over mushrooms. Dot them with all but 2 tablespoons of remaining butter. Sprinkle with bread crumbs and remaining garlic butter. Bake until browned. For individual service, bake in small scallop shells or ramekins.

sea food luncheon

SCALLOPS BAKED IN GARLIC SAUCE   SALAD. Wash, clean, and dry 2 bunches watercress. Cut off stems. Divide into 6 individual salad bowls. Combine 1½ cups chopped celery, 4 cubed peeled and cored apples, ½ cup chopped nuts, and ¾ cup French dressing. Serve over watercress.

BUTTERED TOAST   COFFEE

Sheepshead Bay Casserole

OVEN TIME: 30 MINUTES AT 350°   6-8 SERVINGS

1 large green pepper, seeded and chopped
1 medium onion, chopped
1 cup diced celery
1 cup cooked or canned crab meat, flaked
1 cup cooked or canned shrimp
¾ teaspoon salt
⅛ teaspoon pepper
1 teaspoon A-1 sauce
1 cup mayonnaise
1 cup buttered soft bread crumbs

Gently mix together in a large bowl, green pepper, onion, celery, crab meat, shrimp, salt, pepper, A-1 sauce and mayonnaise. Transfer to greased medium casserole. Sprinkle top with buttered crumbs. Bake until crumbs are golden brown and casserole is bubbling. Serve when you want a superb company dish.

summer buffet

SHEEPSHEAD BAY CASSEROLE   POTATO SALAD BOWL. Combine ½ cup each of cooked diced potatoes, string beans, peas, carrots, cauliflower, and asparagus tips. Let stand in refrigerator in French dressing to cover at least 1 hour. Serve chilled in individual lettuce leaves.   WHOLE WHEAT MUFFINS
TINY PASTRIES   COFFEE

Old Charleston Shrimp and Corn Casserole

OVEN TIME: ½ HOUR AT 300°   4 SERVINGS

2 cups canned or fresh corn kernels, drained
2 eggs, separated
1 tablespoon butter, melted
½ cup milk
1 cup peeled cleaned raw shrimp
Salt and pepper to taste

Combine corn, egg yolks, butter, milk, shrimp, salt and pepper to taste. Stir to blend well. Beat egg whites until stiff, fold them into first mixture, then transfer to small buttered casserole. Bake until pie is set. A delightfully quick one-dish meal.

from South Carolina

No dish can ever equal the one which memory keeps alive, but this old-time casserole comes pretty close.

OLD CHARLESTON SHRIMP AND CORN CASSEROLE   ASPARAGUS SALAD. Spread 4 cooked asparagues leaves over shredded lettuce in individual salad plates. Cut 4 thin slices of Bermuda onion, separate into rings, toss over asparagus. Dress with vinaigrette dressing. (French dressing with 1 teaspoon prepared mustard, ¼ cup chopped dill pickles. Shake well. Add 1 chopped hard-cooked egg.)

BUTTERED BISCUITS   MARMALADE   BEVERAGE

Baked Tuna with Brazil Nuts

OVEN TIME: 15-20 MINUTES AT 350°   4 SERVINGS

4 tablespoons butter
4 tablespoons flour
¾ teaspoon salt
Dash of pepper
2 cups milk
1 13-ounce can tuna fish, drained and flaked (save liquid)
½ teaspoon Worcestershire sauce
¼ cup shredded pimentos
1 cup ground Brazil nuts
6 shelled whole Brazil nuts

Make a sauce: Melt butter, stir in flour, salt and pepper. Gradually add milk, tuna liquid, and Worcestershire sauce. Cook slowly until smooth and thick. Add half of pimentos, ground Brazil nuts, tuna fish. Pour into greased small casserole. Top with remaining pimentos and whole Brazil nuts arranged to make a pretty pattern. Put in oven to bake. A Lenten favorite. (To shell Brazil nuts, put them into 400° oven for 20 minutes. Cook, crack, and shell . . . they come out whole. Or boil in salted water for 3 minutes.)

Lenten luncheon

BAKED TUNA WITH BRAZIL NUTS   DELMONICO POTATO SALAD. Combine 1 cup cooked cubed potatoes, ¼ cup chopped celery, ¼ cup chopped cucumber, ¼ cup mayonnaise, 1 tablespoon vinegar, ½ teaspoon grated onion, salt and pepper to taste.   HOT MUFFINS   COFFEE

Tuna Party Casserole

OVEN TIME: 20-30 MINUTES AT 400°   4 SERVINGS

4 tablespoons butter
½ cup chopped onions
¼ cup chopped green pepper
8-ounce package noodles
1½ teaspoons salt
½ teaspoon pepper
1½ cans condensed cream of mushroom soup, undiluted
1 No. 2 can tomatoes, drained
1 7-ounce can solid pack tuna fish, drained and flaked
¼ teaspoon thyme
1 cup crushed potato chips

1. Melt butter in skillet. Add onions and green pepper, and cook until soft but not brown.
2. Cook noodles in boiling salted water for about 10 minutes until tender.
3. Combine salt, pepper and cream of mushroom soup.
4. In a greased small casserole, spread half the noodles, cover with half the mushroom soup, half the onion-peppers, half the canned tomatoes, and half the tuna. Repeat layers.
5. Sprinkle thyme and potato chips over top and bake until crusty. Good to eat and pretty too.

supper for four

TUNA PARTY CASSEROLE. Do not cover casserole. Top should be crusty.
WALDORF SALAD. Mix 1½ cups cubed peeled apples, 1 cup finely cut celery, ½ cup mayonnaise, ¼ cup chopped pecans. Serve chilled in lettuce leaves.   BRAN MUFFINS   BEVERAGE

BEEF SPECIALTIES FOR YOUR TABLE

Aldilla, Mexican Flank Steak Casserole : Beef Piquante : Normandy Casserole : Corned Beef Hash Moritz : Balkan Hamburger : Nevada Hamburger Casserole : Bitki : Armenian Hamburger Casserole : Cuban Beef and Pepper Casserole : Musaca : Tamale Pie : Braciulini : Carrot and Kugel Casserole : Roast Beef and Sour Cream Casserole : Picadillo : Liver Gulyas

Aldilla, Mexican Flank Steak Casserole

OVEN TIME: 1½ HOURS AT 300°   4 SERVINGS

1 pound flank steak
⅔ cup flour
1 teaspoon salt
1 teaspoon chili powder
2 tablespoons oil
1 small onion, chopped
1 green pepper, seeded and chopped
2 cups chopped tomatoes
¼ cup chili sauce

Wipe steak and cut it into large pieces. Combine flour, salt and chili powder. Pound into steak pieces. Brown them on both sides in hot oil. Remove to casserole. Combine onion, pepper, tomatoes and chili sauce. Pour over flank steak. Cover and bake until very tender. Uncover casserole for last few minutes to thicken sauce. Flank steak is a tough meat but it is well flavored and can be as delicious as the finest steak if baked slowly.

menu for a hearty supper

ALDILLA   POTATO AND CHEESE CASSEROLE. Beat 4 cooked potatoes with ¼ cup butter, ½ cup hot milk, 1 cup grated American cheese, 2 eggs, ½ teaspoon salt. Bake in greased casserole with Aldilla, 30-40 minutes.   LETTUCE AND TOMATO SALAD WITH RUSSIAN DRESSING

TOASTED ROLLS   ICE CREAM WITH FUDGE SAUCE AND SALTED NUTS COFFEE

Beef Piquante

2 pounds boneless beef, cut into chunks
2 large green peppers, seeded and coarsely chopped
2 large Spanish onions, coarsely chopped
4 cups canned tomatoes
1½ teaspoon salt
¼ teaspoon pepper
½ teaspoon sugar
⅔ cup cooked pitted prunes
6 small pared potatoes

Put beef into large casserole and smother with peppers and onions. Combine canned tomatoes, salt, pepper, and sugar. Pour over meat. Surround with prunes and potatoes. Cover and bake until beef is tender. Don't be afraid to keep this casserole in the oven. Longer cooking improves it, but if meat appears to be dry, add beef stock. Don't increase the heat—this casserole needs slow baking.

family supper

BEEF PIQUANTE   CAULIFLOWER AND ANCHOVY SALAD. Cook 2 heads of cauliflower until just tender, not too soft. Separate into flowerets; chill in refrigerator. Combine 6 tablespoons olive and anchovy oil, 2 tablespoons tarragon vinegar, 2 tablespoons grated onion, 3 tablespoons chopped anchovies. Serve over flowerets.   HOT BUTTERED ROLLS

ANGEL FOOD CAKE   BEVERAGE

Normandy Casserole

OVEN TIME: 3-3½ HOURS AT 300°   8 SERVINGS

3-4 pound pot roast of beef (rump, boned chuck or round)
½ cup seasoned flour (1 teaspoon salt and ¼ teaspoon pepper)
3 tablespoons beef drippings or fat
6 small pared potatoes
½ pound dried apricots
1 cup sliced celery
1 cup sliced carrots
1½ teaspoons salt
½ teaspoon pepper
1 teaspoon chopped parsley
1½ cups beef stock

Wipe roast. Roll it in flour. Melt drippings or fat and brown roast on all sides, allowing about 15 minutes for this procedure. Transfer to deep casserole. Surround meat with potatoes, top with a layer each of apricots, celery, and carrots. Season each layer with salt, pepper, and parsley. Pour in beef stock, cover casserole tightly and bake in slow oven until beef is tender. Test it with a fork to be sure it is soft. Remove roast to platter to carve. Put slices back and serve from casserole.

buffet party

NORMANDY CASSEROLE. A wonderful party dish which improves as it waits.   GREEN SALAD FOR EIGHT. Wash, dry and shred 2 heads lettuce, 1 head endive, 1 small peeled cucumber, 2 young carrots, 1 stalk celery, 1 green seeded pepper, 3 scallions; add 3 diced tomatoes, 6 sliced ripe olives, 1 can drained anchovies, and salt and pepper to taste. Serve with French dressing.

PINEAPPLE SHERBET   FRUIT BOWL   COOKIES   BEVERAGE

Corned Beef Hash Moritz

OVEN TIME: 10-15 MINUTES AT 375°   6 SERVINGS

3 tablespoons butter
6 chicken livers, cut in half
1 cup sliced mushrooms
2½ cups chopped cold corned beef
2 cups wine sauce
1 cup grated Swiss cheese
1½ cups seasoned mashed potatoes

Melt half the butter in a frying pan and sauté mushrooms, remove and sauté chicken livers. In a greased medium casserole,
arrange a layer of mushrooms, a layer of corned beef, wine
sauce, and livers. Sprinkle cheese between each layer and on·
top. Shape potatoes into little mounds. Put them around the
edge of the casserole, dot with remaining butter and bake
until potatoes are brown and cheese is puffy.

supper for six

CORNED BEEF HASH MORITZ   WINE SAUCE. Dissolve 1 tablespoon
   cornstarch in ¼ cup cold water, stir in ¾ cup hot water. Cook
   until thick, add 1 cup wine and 1 tablespoon lemon juice.

MIXED GREENS. Just before serving, combine in large bowl 1 head
   crisp lettuce, broken into pieces, 1 cup sliced cucumbers, 3
   tablespoons chopped scallions, 2 cubed tomatoes. Toss with ¾
   cup French dressing.

COCONUT LAYER CAKE   BEVERAGE

Balkan Hamburger

OVEN TIME: 40-50 MINUTES AT 375°   6 SERVINGS

1 medium eggplant, pared
1½ pounds beefsteak, ground twice
1 teaspoon salt
¼ teaspoon pepper
1 clove garlic, minced or chopped fine
3 tablespoons oil
1 small onion, chopped
1½ cups tomato sauce
¼ teaspoon thyme
½ cup fine bread crumbs
3 tablespoons melted butter

Cut eggplant into slices ¼-inch thick. Soak in salted water for 20 minutes. Meanwhile season beef with salt and pepper. Shape into 1-inch balls. Sauté them quickly with garlic in hot oil until brown on all sides. Set aside. Drain and dry eggplant slices. In same frying pan, adding more oil if necessary, brown eggplant and onion. Add tomato sauce and thyme. Bring to boil. Transfer half to deep casserole, top with meat balls, and add remainder of eggplant-tomato mixture. Cover with bread crumbs. Sprinkle with melted butter. Bake uncovered until crusty and brown. Spoon onto plain cooked rice.

hearty supper for six

BALKAN HAMBURGER   FRESHLY COOKED RICE   ONION AND TOMATO SALAD. Slices of Bermuda onion, firm tomato, French dressing. CORN MUFFINS   LEMON TARTS   COFFEE

Nevada Hamburger Casserole

OVEN TIME: 1 HOUR AT 350°   6 SERVINGS

1½ pounds ground beef
½ pound ground fresh pork shoulder
½ cup uncooked rice
1 teaspoon salt
¼ teaspoon pepper
3 tablespoons fat
3 small onions, chopped
2 small carrots, chopped
1 cup canned tomatoes

Combine beef, pork, rice, salt and pepper. Shape into 12 small patties. Brown in skillet in hot fat. Put 2 patties into each of 6 individual casseroles. Combine other ingredients and divide over the patties. Place the casseroles on a cookie sheet (to make removal from oven easier) and bake until done. Serve in individual casseroles. Lucky you—when you serve this easy meal and count the blessings.

lucky luncheon

NEVADA HAMBURGER CASSEROLE   SALAD AND CUCUMBER SOUR CREAM
DRESSING. Combine 1 cup commercial sour cream, 1 crushed garlic clove, 1 teaspoon sugar, ½ teaspoon salt, ¼ cup minced cucumber, 1 teaspoon minced dill, and serve over crisp shredded lettuce.   POTATO CHIPS   BEVERAGE

Bitki

3 slices bread
1 pound ground beefsteak
1 medium onion, finely chopped
1 teaspoon salt
⅛ teaspoon pepper
2 tablespoons butter
1 No. 2 can potatoes, drained
1 cup commercial sour cream

Soak bread in water for 5 minutes. Drain and mix with beef-steak, onion, salt and pepper. Shape into round cakes and sauté in hot butter. Remove meat cakes to small casserole. Brown potatoes in skillet, then arrange them on top of meat. Add sour cream, cover casserole and bake in moderate oven. Serve cakes and potatoes with sauce, right from casserole.

porch supper

FRUIT SALAD. Orange and grapefruit sections, and melon slices, on bed of lettuce.   ORANGE DRESSING. Combine ½ cup salad oil, ½ teaspoon dry mustard, 1 teaspoon paprika. 1 tablespoon cat-sup, and 3 tablespoons orange juice. Shake well.

BITKI   EGGPLANT, CHEESE AND TOMATO CASSEROLE. Cut eggplant in half. Bake or steam until almost done. Remove pulp, leaving thick wall. Chop fine. Sauté 1 minced large onion in butter, add eggplant pulp and 1 cup finely chopped tomatoes. Thicken with fine crumbs, salt and pepper. Fill eggplants with mixture, sprinkle with grated Parmesan cheese and buttered crumbs. Dot with butter. Bake in oven for 15 minutes.   STRAWBERRY PIE   BEVERAGE

Armenian Hamburger Casserole

OVEN TIME: 40-50 MINUTES AT 400°   8 SERVINGS

1 cup crushed wheat (I have bought this at a store in a
    small town, so I hope it is generally available)
2 pounds chopped beefsteak, not too lean
1 medium onion
1½ teaspoons salt
¼ teaspoon pepper
¾ cup butter
½ cup pine nuts (Armenian and Italian stores sell them)

Soak wheat in cold water for 10 minutes. Drain and squeeze
dry. Add to meat. Put through food chopper with onion, using
fine blade. Season with salt and pepper. Brown in half the butter. Spread half the browned beef in a greased medium casserole. Sprinkle with pine nuts. Spread remainder of browned
beef. Dot top with butter. Cut into squares with a sharp knife.
Bake until very brown on top. Serve hot over steamed rice, right
from the casserole. Try adding plump raisins to the rice.

near East special

ARMENIAN HAMBURGER CASSEROLE   PEASANT SALAD. Combine 2
    cup diced cooked potatoes, 1 no. 2 can drained whole beets,
    1 8-ounce can cooked drained peas, 4 chopped scallions, 1
    peeled and chopped cucumber. Add 1 cup French dressing
    with an additional tablespoon vinegar. Refrigerate 1 hour or
    more. Drain. Serve vegetables with mayonnaise on lettuce.
BAKLAVA or GINGER CUP CAKES   COFFEE

Cuban Beef and Pepper Casserole

OVEN TIME: ABOUT 30 MINUTES AT 375°   4 SERVINGS

3 tablespoons fat or oil
2 sweet peppers, seeded and cut into strips
1 pound ground beef
2 eggs
¾ teaspoon salt
¼ teaspoon cayenne pepper
2 cups corn kernels
4 medium tomatoes, sliced thick
¼ cup buttered crumbs

Heat fat, brown peppers and beef. Remove from heat. Stir in eggs, salt, and pepper. In buttered medium casserole, arrange in layers corn, meat and peppers, sliced tomatoes. Top with buttered crumbs. Bake uncovered in moderate oven until piping hot but still juicy.

Saturday supper Mexicano

DAIQUIRI COCKTAILS   CHEESE STRAWS

CUBAN BEEF AND PEPPER CASSEROLE   KIDNEY BEAN SALAD. Combine 2 cups canned kidney beans, 4 chopped hardcooked eggs, 1 cup sweet chopped pickle, ¼ cup finely diced celery, 1 tablespoon minced onion, ½ cup mayonnaise. Chill. Serve in lettuce cups.

CUBAN BAKED BANANAS. Halve 4 bananas, add 1 tablespoon melted butter, ¼ cup brown sugar, 1 tablespoon lime juice. Bake in oven 20 minutes.

FRESH PINEAPPLE   TOASTED ROLLS   HOT CHOCOLATE

Musaca

OVEN TIME: 40-55 MINUTES AT 350°   6 SERVINGS

2 large eggplants
1 pound chopped beefsteak
1 cup chopped onions
6 tablespoons butter
1 teaspoon salt
¼ teaspoon pepper
2 eggs, slightly beaten
¼ cup buttered fine bread crumbs

1. Cut eggplants into slices ½-inch thick. Soak in salted water for 15 minutes.
2. Brown beefsteak and onion in half the butter. Reserve.
3. Dry eggplant. Fry in remaining butter in same pan. Season with salt and pepper.
4. Alternate layers of eggplant and meat-onion mixture in greased casserole. Pour in eggs. Sprinkle with buttered crumbs.
5. Bake uncovered in moderate oven until beef and eggplant are tender and top is crusty. If you are not ready to serve, cover casserole so it does not dry out. Add beef stock if it is needed.

meal in one oven

MUSACA   POTATO CASSEROLE. Combine 4 cups cooked diced potatoes, 1 diced small onion, 1 cup commercial sour cream, 2 teaspoons salt, ½ teaspoon pepper. Put into greased small casserole, same time and temperature as musaca.

APRICOT UPSIDE-DOWN CAKE. Follow standard recipe for upside-down cake, making 6 servings, but use 8 fresh or canned apricots, cut in half. Bake in oven with rest of meal. Serve with hard sauce or plain cream.   BEVERAGE

Tamale Pie

OVEN TIME: 20-30 MINUTES AT 400°   8-10 SERVINGS

2 cups yellow corn meal
1 teaspoon salt
½ teaspoon black pepper
3 tablespoons butter
3 tablespoons olive oil
½ cup chopped onions
2 pounds chopped beefsteak or cooked diced pork
10-ounce can condensed tomato soup
½ cup stuffed halved olives
1 tablespoon chili powder

1. Pour 1 cup cold water into corn meal to make mush. Boil 4½ cups water, stir in corn-meal mush, salt and pepper. Cook over low heat for several minutes until thick, stirring frequently. Remove from heat and add butter.
2. Heat oil in large skillet, brown onions and meat. Add tomato soup, olives, and chili powder. Cook 10 minutes more. Taste and add more chili if you want a hotter pie.
3. Pour half the cooked corn meal into a shallow buttered casserole. Add meat mixture and top with remaining corn meal. Bake uncovered until steaming hot. Serve as a main dish.

on a summer evening

TAMALE PIE. May be made in the morning and reheated just before serving with no loss of flavor.   CRISP RAW RELISHES. On large platter or lazy Susan arrange chilled washed endive leaves, cut-up romaine lettuce, carrot sticks, radish fans, canned pimento slices, scallions, stuffed olives. Have a bowl of French dressing near.   FRESH PINEAPPLE FINGERS OR SLICES   ICED COFFEE

Braciulini

½ pound ground beef
1 clove garlic, finely minced
3 tablespoons olive oil
1 No. 2½ can Italian plum tomatoes
1 large can water
½ can Italian tomato paste
1 teaspoon salt
1 teaspoon sugar
Dash of orégano
Dash of crushed Italian red peppers
2 pounds shoulder or round steak, sliced ½ inch thick

1. Brown ground beef and garlic in large saucepan in 1 table-spoon hot oil until beef loses its red color. Discard garlic.
2. Add tomatoes, water (measured in large can), tomato paste, salt, sugar, orégano, and pepper. Bring to boil, cover and simmer half an hour.
3. Meanwhile wipe steak. Cut into strips about 1½ inches wide. Roll strips from the short side as tightly as possible. Secure with toothpicks.
4. Brown beef rolls in remaining oil, turning so they brown all over. Transfer to shallow casserole.
5. When sauce is cooked, pour over beef, cover and bake until sauce is very thick and beef is tender.

Italian dinner

BRACIULINI   COOKED MACARONI SHELLS   DANDELION SALAD
CHIANTI WINE   ICE CREAM   CAFÉ ESPRESSO OR COFFEE

Carrot and Kugel Casserole

OVEN TIME: ABOUT 2 HOURS AT 350°   6 SERVINGS

2 pounds carrots, cut into slices ¼-inch thick
1 tablespoon grated onion
2 large sweet potatoes, cut into chunks
1 pound chuck or round steak, cut into 1-inch cubes
½ cup honey
1 tablespoon lemon juice
1 cup sifted all-purpose flour
1 teaspoon baking powder
1 teaspoon salt
¼ teaspoon pepper
⅓ cup rendered chicken fat or shortening
3 tablespoons cold water

1. In a saucepan, combine carrots, onion, sweet potatoes, and steak. Cover with boiling salted water. Simmer for 10 minutes.
2. Turn vegetables, meat, and liquid in which they cooked into a greased large casserole. Combine honey and lemon juice and pour into casserole.
3. Make the kugel (or pudding): Sift flour, baking powder, salt and pepper. Cut in fat with a pastry blender or knife. Add cold water, mixing with a fork. Gather dough lightly into a ball.
4. Put the ball of dough in center of casserole resting in a bed of carrots, sweet potatoes, and steak. Cover and bake until meat is tender. Take off cover and continue baking for 10 minutes until top is deep brown. A hearty dish with unusual flavor.

with an old country flavor

CARROT AND KUGEL CASSEROLE   SALAD. On a bed of broken crisp lettuce pieces, spoon 3 tablespoons cooked drained peas which have been mixed with mayonnaise. Put alternate slices of tomato and hardcooked egg around the border. Brush with more mayonnaise. Serve chilled.

BABKA OR YEAST CAKE   BEVERAGE

Roast Beef and Sour Cream Casserole

OVEN TIME: 20 MINUTES AT 375°   6 SERVINGS

2 cups leftover roast beef, chopped coarsely
2 cups cooked rice
1 teaspoon salt
Dash of pepper
1½ cups mushroom soup
½ cup thin cream
2 tablespoons butter
1 cup commercial sour cream
Dash of paprika

Set aside ¼ cup rice for the topping. Arrange a layer of roast beef and a layer of rice in a greased medium casserole. Sprinkle with salt and pepper. Repeat roast beef and rice layers. Combine mushroom soup and thin cream and pour over meat. Sprinkle with remaining rice. Dot with butter. Bake in moderate oven until slightly brown on top, about 15 minutes. Spoon sour cream into casserole, sprinkle with paprika and put back in oven until sour cream is heated through. Serve right from casserole— and be glad that you roasted a beef large enough for leftovers.

potpourri party buffet

MASHED AVOCADO AND ONION DIP   COCKTAIL CRACKERS   SHERRY
ROAST BEEF AND SOUR CREAM CASSEROLE   SALAD MUSCOVY. Combine
1½ cups mixed cooked vegetables (frozen ones are fine, cook them first) 2 apples which have been pared, cored and diced, and ¼ cup chopped salt herring. Mix with mayonnaise thinned with vinegar. Refrigerate for 1 hour. Serve on shredded lettuce.
KASHA. Cook buckwheat groats as directed on package.
BROWN BREAD   FRESH FRUIT   BEVERAGE

Picadillo

OVEN TIME: 20-25 MINUTES AT 400°   6 SERVINGS

½ cup chopped sweet onions
¼ cup chopped sweet pepper
1 clove garlic, minced
3 tablespoons butter or oil
2 cups chopped tomatoes
1½ cups chopped cooked beef
½ cup beef stock or bouillon cube dissolved in hot water
1 teaspoon salt
1 teaspoon vinegar
1 bay leaf, broken into small pieces
Dash of cloves

Cook onions, pepper, and garlic in hot butter or oil until soft. Add tomatoes and let stew for ten minutes. Now put in beef, beef stock, salt, vinegar, bay leaf, and cloves. Stir to blend ingredients. Turn into a small casserole and put into oven until well baked and savory. Cubans serve Picadillo at noon with cooked rice, fried bananas, and fried eggs. I like it as a late supper after an evening of bridge.

for a late supper

PICADILLO   PINEAPPLE AND AVOCADO SALAD. Cut 3 unpeeled avocados in half. Remove seed. Scoop out half the pulp. Mash and combine with 1 cup crushed pineapple. Mix with ½ cup French dressing. Fill halves. Serve over crushed ice or well chilled.

GUAVA PASTE OR JAM AND CRACKERS   COFFEE

Liver Gulyas

1 pound beef or calf liver
½ small onion
½ green pepper
1 cup fine bread crumbs
¾ teaspoon salt
¼ teaspoon pepper
½ pound fresh or canned mushrooms
4 tablespoons butter
4 tablespoons flour
1½ cups beef stock or consommé
1 No. 2 can new potatoes, drained
½ teaspoon Hungarian paprika

1. Pour boiling water over liver. Drain at once. Discard skin
and membrane. Put liver twice through food chopper with
onion and green pepper, using fine blade. Combine ground mixture with bread crumbs, salt and pepper.
2. In hot butter, brown mushrooms, stirring to brown all over.
Add more butter to pan, stir in flour, beef stock, or consommé.
Bring to boil, then let simmer for 5 minutes. Pour sauce over
liver in casserole, put potatoes around as a border, sprinkle with
paprika and bake uncovered until liver is done and potatoes are·
browned. Serve with cooked noodles.

dinner Hungarian style

LIVER GULYAS   NOODLE AND GREEN PEPPER SALAD. Cut 4 green peppers into long thin strips. Cook in small amount of water. Toss
with 2 cups cooked buttered noodles. Combine ½ cup olive oil
and 3 tablespoons vinegar. Sprinkle over salad. Refrigerate
several hours before serving.   BACON BISCUITS
FRUIT COMPOTE   COFFEE

GOURMET VEAL CASSEROLES

Djuvee : Veal Divannini : Veal Paprikas : Vitello Forno : Ghivetch Bucaresti : Swedish Veal and Orange Casserole : Veal Parmigiana : Veal and Noodles en Casserole

Djuvee

OVEN TIME: 1½ HOURS AT 325°   4-6 SERVINGS

2 medium onions, diced
1 large green pepper, diced
2 tablespoons olive oil or lard
1 cup uncooked rice
3 large tomatoes, diced
3 large potatoes, diced
1 pound uncooked pork and veal, cut into bite-size pieces
1 teaspoon salt
¼ teaspoon pepper
2 cups beef stock or water
Dash of paprika

1. Cook onions and pepper in hot oil in frying pan. Remove and brown separately first the rice, then potatoes, then meat.
2. In a greased large casserole, put browned onion and peppers, half the tomatoes, potatoes, rice, remaining tomatoes and finally the browned meat. Sprinkle salt and pepper between layers.
3. Pour in beef stock or water, cover and bake slowly until all the liquid is absorbed and the vegetables are tender. Serve hot sprinkled with paprika. A favorite Yugoslavian stew, frequently baked with fish instead of pork and veal.

peasant party

DJUVEE   STRING BEANS VINAIGRETTE. Cook string beans until tender but do not overcook. Drain and cool. Let stand in ½ cup vinaigrette dressing (to standard French dressing add chopped sweet pickle, parsley, and green pepper). Refrigerate at least 1 hour.

APPLE CAKE   BRANDY AND COFFEE

Veal Divannini

OVEN TIME: 20 MINUTES AT 400°   6 SERVINGS

2 cups white sauce made with cream instead of milk
1 cup cooked veal, cut into thin strips
6 ounces spaghetti, cooked and cut up
1 cup cooked asparagus pieces
½ cup mushrooms, sliced and sautéed in butter
1 egg yolk, slightly beaten
⅓ cup grated Parmesan cheese
¾ cup buttered cracker crumbs

Combine sauce, veal, spaghetti, asparagus and mushrooms. Heat. Remove from flame and stir in egg. Turn into buttered large casserole or individual ramekins. Sprinkle with cheese and crumbs and bake in hot oven until browned on top and bubbly hot. Be a clever hostess—prepare this in the morning, ready to pop into the oven half an hour or so before guests are due.

Saturday night buffet

VEAL DIVANNINI   SALAD PLATE. Tomato chunks, cucumber fingers, black and green olives, radishes, pimentos.

BRANDIED PEACHES. Put 12 canned peach halves in baking dish, cut side up. Combine 2 tablespoons butter, 3 tablespoons apricot or peach brandy. Divide into peach cups. Bake 10 minutes.

PETIT FOURS   COFFEE

Veal Paprikas

OVEN TIME: 2 HOURS AT 350°   6-8 SERVINGS

2 pounds boned shoulder of veal, cut 2x2x1 inches
2 cloves garlic, crushed or pressed
¼ cup butter
½ cup chopped carrots
½ cup chopped celery
¼ cup chopped pimentos
¼ cup chopped green pepper
¼ cup chopped onions
2 tablespoons flour
1 cup beef stock or bouillon cube dissolved in hot water
3 tablespoons tomato paste
2 cups commercial sour cream
2 tablespoons sweet paprika
1 teaspoon salt

1. Brown veal and garlic in saucepan in hot butter, turning pieces once. Transfer to casserole, but discard garlic.
2. To butter remaining in saucepan, add carrots, celery, pimentos, green pepper, and onions. Cook about 5 minutes until vegetables are just soft; they should not be brown.
3. Stir in flour, pour in beef stock, tomato paste, and sour cream. Cook slowly until sauce begins to thicken. Add paprika and salt.
4. Pour sauce over veal in casserole, cover and bake until meat and vegetables are tender. Serve with delicious juices—this is a fragrant company casserole.

simple and super

VEAL PAPRIKAS   MIXED GREEN SALAD WITH FRENCH DRESSING
TOASTED HERB BREAD. Cut loaf of bread into slices almost to bottom. Mix soft butter with finely chopped parsley. Spread between slices. Put bread in bag, heat in oven 15 minutes.

Vitello Forno

OVEN TIME: ABOUT 1 HOUR AT 350°   4 SERVINGS

1 pound boneless veal, sliced thin
3 tablespoons butter or margarine
1½ cups thinly sliced potatoes
1 cup green pepper strips, about 1-inch wide
¾ teaspoon salt
¼ teaspoon pepper
2 cloves garlic, finely minced or crushed
2 cups tomato sauce

Have butcher flatten veal or pound it yourself to ¼-inch thickness. Cut into 2-inch squares. Brown both sides in hot butter in a saucepan on top of the stove (or in oven heated to 450°). Set meat squares aside as they brown. In medium casserole, arrange a layer of browned veal, a layer of sliced potatoes, a layer of peppers. Season each layer with salt, pepper, and bits of garlic. Pour tomato sauce on top, cover and bake until everything is tender. When you serve this savory veal, potato, and pepper casserole you will know why Italian cooking is so popular.

Italian style dinner

ANTIPASTO. Italian ham, salami, beets, cooked cauliflower, anchovies; olive oil and lemon juice dressing.

VITELLO FORNO   ARTICHOKES LUIGI. Cook 4 artichokes in boiling salted water for 15 minutes. Spread leaves, remove chokes. Sauté 1 pound sliced mushrooms in oil, add ½ cup dry crumbs, 2 finely chopped garlic cloves, 1 tablespoon chopped parsley, salt and pepper. Put between leaves. Stand in casserole, pour in water from sides until 1-inch deep, bake uncovered about 50 minutes.

ITALIAN BREAD   FRUIT AND CHEESE PLATTER   COFFEE

Ghivetch Bucaresti

OVEN TIME: 1½ HOURS AT 375°   4 SERVINGS

4 veal cutlets, about 2 pounds
3 tablespoons butter
6 small tomatoes
1 teaspoon salt
Dash of crushed Tabasco pepper
1 small eggplant, diced
1 cup sliced onions
1 cup sliced mushrooms
1 package frozen string beans
1 cup tomato juice
1 cup beef stock or bouillon cube dissolved in hot water

1. Pound cutlets with a mallet or edge of a plate until they are flattened to about ¼-inch thickness. Brown them slowly on both sides in butter in a large skillet. Now transfer cutlets to large casserole.
2. Cut tomatoes into thick slices and put on top of browned veal. Sprinkle with some of the salt and Tabasco.
3. Brown eggplant, onions, and mushrooms in skillet, adding more butter if necessary. Put over veal with string beans. Season with more salt and Tabasco.
4. Bring tomato juice and beef stock to quick boil in same skillet, stirring to pick up little bits of meat which stick to pan. Pour into casserole, cover and bake until veal and vegetables are tender. Serve this colorful Romanian dish in the casserole in which it was baked.

winter supper

GHIVETCH BUCARESTI	CORN-MEAL BREAD
COMPOTE OF FRUIT	BEVERAGE

Swedish Veal and Orange Casserole

OVEN TIME: 1½ HOURS AT 325°   8-10 SERVINGS

3 pounds veal cutlets, sliced thin
½ cup grated Parmesan cheese
1 tablespoon salt
1 teaspoon pepper
1 teaspoon sugar
3 tablespoons butter
2 cups sliced carrots
3 oranges, peeled and sliced thick
1 cup beef stock
4 tablespoons orange juice or sherry

Pound cutlets until thin. Combine cheese, salt, pepper, and sugar. Sprinkle over veal. Melt butter in skillet and brown veal on both sides. Transfer to buttered shallow casserole. Put carrots and orange slices over veal. Pour in beef stock, cover and bake about 45 minutes. Now add orange juice and bake 20 minutes more until veal is tender. Veal and oranges are a remarkably good combination with cooked cauliflower.

Swedish style supper

SMORGASBORD. Chopped liver, chopped cooked beets, herring slices, string beans with chopped onions, devilled eggs.
CHILLED AQUAVIT
SWEDISH VEAL AND ORANGE CASSEROLE   COOKED CAULIFLOWER
CRISP RYE BREAD   PASTRIES   BEVERAGE

Veal Parmigiana

OVEN TIME: 1½ HOURS AT 300°   4 SERVINGS

1 pound boneless veal
4 tablespoons olive oil
¼ cup sliced mushrooms
2 cloves garlic, finely crushed
Salt and pepper
1 teaspoon dried rosemary
½ cup marsala or sherry wine
½ cup grated Parmesan cheese

Have the butcher pound the veal, or flatten it yourself with a mallet, until it is no more than ¼ inch thick. Cut it into neat pieces, about 3 inches square. Quickly brown them in a skillet in hot oil, turning once. Put them into a greased shallow casserole as they brown. In same oil in which veal was sautéed, cook mushrooms and garlic until soft on both sides. Transfer mushrooms to casserole. Discard garlic. Bring wine, rosemary, salt and pepper to quick boil in skillet. Pour into casserole (with any bits of veal or vegetables which were left in the pan). Sprinkle cheese on top, cover and bake until veal is very tender. Serve to friends who are either peasants or poets—this meal has universal appeal.

latin buffet

ANTIPASTO   BREADSTICKS

VEAL PARMIGIANA   COOKED SPAGHETTI WITH ANCHOVY SAUCE

ALMOND STUFFED PEACHES. Combine ¼ cup cake crumbs, ¼ cup finely ground almonds, 1 teaspoon grated orange rind, 3 tablespoons sugar, ½ cup sherry wine. Fill 8 peach halves with mixture. Bake in oven in shallow casserole about 40 minutes.

Veal and Noodles en Casserole

OVEN TIME: 45 MINUTES AT 300°   6 SERVINGS

2 pounds veal cut into 2″ pieces
¼ cup seasoned flour (2 teaspoons salt, ¼ teaspoon pepper)
5 tablespoons butter
1 cup chopped onion
1 cup water
8 ounces noodles
1 cup mushrooms
1 cup commercial sour cream
¼ cup buttered bread crumbs

1. Dip veal in seasoned flour. Brown in hot butter. Add onions and water, and cook slowly about 45 minutes.
2. Cook noodles in boiling salted water until soft. About 8 minutes. Drain.
3. Combine veal and noodles. Add mushrooms and sour cream. Turn into greased medium casserole. Top with crumbs. Cover and bake in slow oven until veal is tender. This is one of these clever little dishes, made ahead to look easy and keep you unruffled before dinner.

hot weather supper

VEAL AND NOODLES EN CASSEROLE   TOMATOES FILLED WITH GREEN PEAS. Dip 6 tomatoes of same size in hot, then cold, water to remove skin. Scoop out pulp, leaving thick wall. Combine cold cooked peas with mayonnaise and bit of tomato pulp. Fill shells. Sprinkle hardcooked chopped egg on top, spread with mayonnaise, put handful of cooked peas around as a beaded border. Serve cold.   PARKER HOUSE ROLLS
CHILLED APPLE SAUCE COMBINED WITH CRUSHED PINEAPPLE   BEVERAGE

LAMB CASSEROLES EVERYONE LOVES

Kibbi, A Baked Lamb Casserole : Lamb and Vegetable Medley : Syrian Lamb Pilau : Lahmajoon : Lamb Chops in Grape Jelly : Casserole of Lamb, Apples and Onions

Kibbi, a Baked Lamb Casserole

OVEN TIME: 1 HOUR AT 375°   6-8 SERVINGS

2 pounds boned lamb
½ cup finely chopped onion
1 teaspoon salt
¼ teaspoon pepper
1 cup cracked wheat
Ice water
¼ cup shelled pine nuts
¼ cup butter

1. Have lamb ground at the store. Combine with onion, salt, and pepper.
2. Soak wheat in cold water for 15 minutes. Drain and squeeze dry.
3. Put ground lamb and wheat through the meat grinder together, or chop very well. Sprinkle mixture with enough ice water to make it moist and soft.
4. Spread mixture into well greased shallow casserole with a sharp knife, cut it into diamonds or squares.
5. Sprinkle with pine nuts, dot with butter, and bake until golden.
6. Run knife around each diamond or square, lift out and serve hot.

Mediterranean specialty

KIBBI   CHOPPED EGGPLANT SALAD. Bake 1 large eggplant until soft. Cool. Remove skin and some of seeds. Chop pulp fine with 1 medium onion. Season with olive oil, salt, pepper. Serve with sliced tomatoes, black olives, pimento shreds.   BLACK BREAD
CHERRY TARTS   COFFEE

Lamb and Vegetable Medley

OVEN TIME: 1½ HOURS AT 350°   6 SERVINGS

2 cups cooked lamb cut into bite-size pieces
1 cup diced beets, drained
1 cup diced onions
2 cups sliced potatoes
1 parsnip, sliced
1 teaspoon salt
¼ teaspoon pepper
¼ teaspoon powdered thyme
¼ teaspoon powdered marjoram
2 cups lamb stock made from bones or gravy, or water

Put lamb pieces into buttered medium casserole. Arrange vegetables around them, keeping each kind together. Sprinkle with salt, pepper, thyme and marjoram. Pour in lamb stock or water. Cover casserole and bake until lamb is tender and browned. Add more liquid if necessary. Do be sure to use the beets in the recipe as they add just the right taste and texture. Filling enough to serve on nippy evenings when everyone is ravenous.

supper delight

LAMB AND VEGETABLE MEDLEY   PINEAPPLE-CHEESE SALAD. Cover 6 slices of canned pineapple with French dressing. Let stand 1 hour. Drain. Dip borders in finely chopped parsley or mint. Arrange on individual plates over shredded lettuce. Fill centers with mounds of cream cheese rolled in grated nuts.

HOT SEEDED ROLLS   LEMON MERINGUE PIE   BEVERAGE

Syrian Lamb Pilau

OVEN TIME: 25-30 MINUTES AT 375°   6 SERVINGS

3 cups cooked diced lamb
3 cups cooked rice
3 small tomatoes, finely chopped
1½ tablespoons chopped onions
Salt and pepper to taste
1½ cups lamb or other meat stock
½ cup buttered fine bread crumbs

In a generously greased medium casserole, arrange alterate layers of lamb, rice, and tomatoes. Season each layer with chopped onion, salt, and pepper. Repeat layers until all ingredients are used. Pour in stock. Top with buttered crumbs. Bake uncovered until brown and bubbly. This is a simple recipe for a well-flavored Near East specialty.

supper for six

SYRIAN LAMB PILAU   MUSHROOM CASSEROLE. Slice 1½ pounds mushrooms. Sauté in hot butter, add ½ cup chicken stock and cook 10 minutes. Stir in 2 tablespoons lemon juice, salt and pepper. Remove from heat, add beaten egg yolk and a tablespoon sherry. Put into casserole, dot with butter and bake for 10 minutes.

CHILLED CANTALOUPE HALVES WITH SEEDLESS GRAPES   COFFEE

Lahmajoon

2 cups sifted all-purpose flour
3 teaspoons baking powder
1 teaspoon salt
6 tablespoons shortening
⅔ cup milk
Dash of onion juice
3 tablespoons olive oil
1 pound lamb, finely ground
1½ cups chopped onions
1½ cups tomato pulp or finely chopped tomatoes
2 tablespoons chopped parsley
1 teaspoon salt
¼ teaspoon pepper

1. Make biscuit dough: Sift together flour, baking powder, salt.
Cut in shortening. Quickly stir in milk and onion juice. Roll out
dough ½- to ¾-inch thick on floured board. Cut into ten circles,
each about 5 inches in diameter, using a large biscuit cutter or
saucer. Arrange biscuits on baking sheet, not quite touching
each other.
2. Heat olive oil, brown lamb and onions. Spoon out from
saucepan, leaving as much oil as possible.
3. Add tomato pulp, parsley, salt and pepper to pan. Bring to
quick boil. Combine half of this sauce with all of the lamb and
onions.
4. Divide lamb-tomato mixture over biscuits, piling high in the
center. Do not spread out to edges or mixture will run over biscuits.
5. Bake until lamb and biscuits are done.
6. Heat remaining tomato sauce. Pour hot sauce over biscuits
and meat. Allow 2 biscuits as main course; 1 otherwise.

Lamb Chops in Grape Jelly

OVEN TIME: ABOUT 1¼ HOURS AT 375°   6 SERVINGS

6 thick lamb chops
¼ cup flour
2 tablespoons fat
1 teaspoon salt
¼ teaspoon pepper
¼ teaspoon celery salt
3 small onions, quartered
1 carrot, cut into 1-inch slices
¾ cup grape jelly
¾ cup beef stock or water
1 bay leaf
4 fresh sprigs of parsley
1 whole clove
5 whole peppercorns

1. Trim fat off lamb chops. Wipe meat. Roll in flour. Brown on both sides in hot fat.
2. Transfer browned chops to greased medium casserole. Season them with part of the salt, pepper, and celery salt.
3. Surround chops with onions and carrot slices. Season again with salt, pepper, and celery salt.
4. Combine grape jelly, beef stock or water, bay leaf, parsley, clove and peppercorns. Pour into casserole. Cover and bake until lamb chops are tender and saucy. This is a wonderful way to serve lamb chops.

spring supper

LAMB CHOPS IN GRAPE JELLY   MASHED POTATOES   SALAD OF SEASONAL GREENS   ROQUEFORT FRENCH DRESSING. Crumble 2 tablespoons Roquefort cheese into French dressing. Put over greens just before serving.   HARD FRENCH ROLLS   COFFEE

Casserole of Lamb, Apples and Onions

OVEN TIME: 15 MINUTES AT 450°; 1½ HOURS AT 325°   6 SERVINGS

2 pounds boneless lamb as for stew
¼ cup flour seasoned with salt and pepper
4 tart apples, pared, cored and quartered
12 small white onions, partly cooked
1 cup lamb stock or water
2 tablespoons butter

Wipe lamb. Cut it into 1-inch cubes. Shake a few pieces at a time in a paper bag with flour. Brown in a greased 1½-quart casserole in a hot oven (or on top of stove, then transfer to casserole). Turn pieces so they brown on all sides. Put apple quarters and whole onions around the lamb, pour in lamb stock or water, dot with butter, cover casserole tightly, reduce oven heat to 325° and bake for about 1½ hours. Lamb will be *very* tender.

supper for six

CASSEROLE OF LAMB, APPLES AND ONIONS   POTATOES ANNA. Cut 6 potatoes into thin rounds. Use part to line small buttered casserole. Chop rest of potatoes and put into middle of casserole. Season with salt and pepper, and melted butter combined with a dash of prepared mustard. Bake 50 minutes until potatoes are soft. Remove cover for last 15 minutes to crispen.   BUTTER-MILK ROLLS   ALMOND CRESCENTS   COFFEE

HAM AND PORK FAVORITES

Sweet Potato Pork Pie : Pennsylvania Dutch Spareribs, Sauer-
kraut, and Dumplings : Danish Pork Chops and Fruit : Deep-
Dish Ham and Apple Pie : Upside-Down Ham and Pineapple
Loaf : Pork Chops Baked in Orange Sauce : Ham and Cauli-
flower Polonaise : Spareribs and Sauerkraut Maui : Pork Ten-
derloin with Prunes : Chuck Wagon Hot Pots : Pork Chops
and Rice Casserole

Sweet Potato Pork Pie

OVEN TIME: 30 MINUTES AT 450°   6 SERVINGS

1½ pounds pork
1 bay leaf
3 peppercorns
2 teaspoons salt
¼ cup sliced celery
1 teaspoon chopped parsley
1 cup chopped onions
2 tablespoons fat or shortening
2 tablespoons flour
1 cup pork stock
3 tart apples, pared and sliced thin

Sweet Potato Crust:
1 cup sifted all-purpose flour
3 teaspoons baking powder
1½ teaspoons salt
3 tablespoons shortening
1 cup mashed sweet potatoes
¼ cup milk

Cut pork into 2-inch pieces, pour on enough water to cover, add bay leaf, peppercorns, salt, celery and parsley and cook until pork is done. Strain. Boil liquid down to make 1 cup stock. Cook onions in fat until soft but not brown. Add flour, gradually stir in stock. Cook until smooth and thick. Arrange alternate layers of pork and apples in a greased large casserole. Make crust: Sift together flour, baking powder, and salt. Cut in shortening. Add sweet potatoes and milk to make soft dough. Knead for about a minute. Roll out ½-inch thick, cut out with small biscuit cutter or plate and arrange on pork. Bake until brown and steaming hot. A favorite Southern specialty.

Pennsylvania Dutch Spareribs, Sauerkraut, and Dumplings

OVEN TIME: 2 HOURS AT 350°   4-6 SERVINGS

3 pounds spareribs
1 quart sauerkraut
2 cups all-purpose flour
1 teaspoon baking powder
1 egg, slightly beaten
1 teaspoon salt
¼ teaspoon pepper

Put the spareribs, cut into serving pieces, into a shallow casserole. Spread sauerkraut on top, cover and bake for one and one-half hours. Combine flour, baking powder, egg, salt, and pepper. Drop onto sauerkraut, cover pan and continue baking for 30 minutes longer. This will serve 4 in the Pennsylvania Dutch tradition of plenty, but might be stretched to 6 for less hearty appetites.

Lancaster County buffet

HOT TOMATO SOUP WITH RICE

PENNSYLVANIA DUTCH SPARERIBS, SAUERKRAUT & DUMPLINGS

MASHED POTATOES   APPLE AND CELERY SALAD. Core and dice 4 eating apples, cover with French dressing made with lemon juice rather than vinegar. Add 2 cups sliced celery and 1 cup chopped walnuts. Serve in lettuce cups covered with mayonnaise.

TRAYS OF ASSORTED BREADS AND RELISHES   APPLE PIE AND ICE CREAM

Danish Pork Chops and Fruit

OVEN TIME: 1 HOUR AT 350°   8 SERVINGS

8 pork chops
2 tablespoons flour
2 cups milk
1 teaspoon sugar
1 teaspoon salt
½ teaspoon ground ginger
¼ teaspoon pepper
8 large cooked prunes
2 apples, pared, cored and quartered

Brown chops in frying pan on both sides until golden. Use low heat as pork gets tough if cooked too quickly. Drain off all but two tablespoons fat. Blend in flour, milk, sugar, salt, ginger, and pepper to make a smooth sauce. Cook until sauce thickens. Put browned chops in casserole, pour on sauce, surround with prunes and apples, cover and bake one hour until chops are tender. Lots of good flavor in this Danish casserole.

Danish holiday dinner

SMORREBROD. Danish appetizers of smoked salmon canapés, cucumber fingers, caviar, brown bread, onion rings.

DANISH PORK CHOPS AND FRUIT   BROWNED POTATOES. Put 8 parboiled potatoes into casserole with butter. Bake tender about 50 minutes.

DANISH RED CABBAGE. Shred fine 3 red cabbages, removing outer leaves. Add ¼ cup shredded onions, 2 cups pared thin-sliced apples. Put into saucepan, cover with boiling salted water and cook until cabbage is tender. Drain. Add ¼ cup vinegar, 3 tablespoons butter, salt, pepper, and ¾ cup grape jelly. Cook 10 minutes longer. Serve hot.

RYE BREAD   ASSORTED PASTRIES   BEVERAGES

Deep-Dish Ham and Apple Pie

OVEN TIME: 10 MINUTES AT 450°; 20 MINUTES AT 350°   6 SERVINGS

5 tart apples, pared and cored
3 cups cooked chopped ham
¼ cup brown sugar
2 tablespoons lemon juice
2 tablespoons melted butter
Pastry for 1-crust pie (rolled to fit casserole you are using)

1. Cut apples as for apple pie. Be sure not to slice too thin.
2. Spread a layer of ham in a generously greased casserole. Cover with a layer of apples.
3. Sprinkle with brown sugar (the amount depends on the tartness of the apples) and lemon juice.
4. Repeat layers of ham and apples, ending with apples. Dot with butter.
5. Cover with pastry, moistening edge with water so crust sticks to baking dish. Bake at 450° for 10 minutes; reduce heat to 350 and bake 20-30 minutes more or until pie is done. A handsome pie you'll be proud to serve.

old-fashioned country spread

DEEP DISH HAM AND APPLE PIE   MACARONI SALAD. Combine 4 cups cooked (½ pound uncooked) elbow macaroni, 1 cup celery slices, ½ cup sliced scallions, ½ cup sliced stuffed olives, 2 tablespoons chopped pimento, 1 teaspoon salt, dash pepper, 1 cup mayonnaise, 2 teaspoons lemon juice. Chill for several hours. Decorate with slivers of American cheese.

BLUEBERRY PIE   COFFEE

Upside-Down Ham and Pineapple Loaf

OVEN TIME: ABOUT 1 HOUR AT 375°   6 SERVINGS

¼ cup butter
¼ cup brown sugar
6 slices canned drained pineapple
½ cup maraschino cherries, drained
1½ pounds ground raw ham
1½ cups soft bread crumbs
2 eggs, slightly beaten

Melt butter in a shallow casserole which is flameproof. Stir in sugar. Arrange pineapple slices and maraschino cherries close together in a pretty pattern on the sugar. Mix ham, crumbs, and eggs. Press mixture onto fruit. Bake until top browns. Pour off fat as it accumulates. To serve, invert on heated platter so fruit side is up. Press back any pieces which may fall off when you turn the loaf. Here's a pie to be the pivot of your buffet table.

supper buffet Sunday

UPSIDE-DOWN HAM AND PINEAPPLE LOAF   BEST EVER COLE SLAW. Grind coarsely in food chopper 1 firm head of cabbage and 5 stalks of cleaned celery. Add ¼ teaspoon salt, dash of pepper, 1 tablespoon vinegar. Refrigerate several hours. Combine 6 tablespoons mayonnaise, 3 tablespoons bottled relish or chopped sweet pickles, and 1 chopped hardcooked egg. Put over cabbage just before serving with strips of pimento.

RYE BREAD AND ROLLS   ASSORTED FINGER PASTRIES   COFFEE

Pork Chops Baked in Orange Sauce

OVEN TIME: 50-60 MINUTES AT 350°   6 SERVINGS

6 thick loin pork chops
1 teaspoon salt
¼ teaspoon pepper
1 small onion
¼ cup chopped celery
Pinch of thyme
1 cup orange juice
2 tablespoons wine vinegar

Brown chops in skillet on both sides, allowing about 10 minutes. Sprinkle with salt and pepper. Transfer to greased medium casserole. In a minimum amount of the fat left from the chops, brown onion and celery. Turn onto chops. Combine other ingredients, sprinkle over chops in casserole, cover and bake until meat is tender. Remove cover for last 10 minutes to thicken sauce. A delightfully easy one-dish meal which will please your dinner guests.

guestworthy dinner

PORK CHOPS BAKED IN ORANGE SAUCE   BOULANGERE POTATOES. Pare and slice thin 8 potatoes. Put into shallow casserole with 2 onions, thinly sliced. Top with 3 tablespoons butter, ½ teaspoon salt, 1 pinch pepper. Pour in 1 cup boiling beef stock (made with bouillon cube) or water. Cook same time as potatoes until they are soft and crusty on top.   MIXED GREEN SALAD WITH FRENCH DRESSING

HOT MUFFINS   STRAWBERRY SHORTCAKE   COFFEE

Ham and Cauliflower Polonaise

OVEN TIME: 15-20 MINUTES AT 400°   4-6 SERVINGS

1½ cups soft bread crumbs
1½ cups milk
2 tablespoons butter
Salt and pepper
1 head cooked or 1 package frozen cauliflower
1½ cups cooked chopped ham
2 hard-cooked eggs, mashed
1 tablespoon chopped parsley

Add bread crumbs to milk and cook over low flame, stirring until smooth. Remove from heat. Stir in butter, salt and pepper. Separate cauliflower into flowerets. In a greased medium casserole, put alternate layers of flowerets, bread sauce, and ham. Repeat layers. Combine eggs and parsley and spread on top. Cover and bake until golden. A lovely dish, even if it is composed mainly of leftovers.

country dinner

HAM AND CAULIFLOWER POLONAISE   SEASONAL SALAD WITH SLICED MUSHROOMS. Tear 1 or 2 heads of seasonal lettuce into pieces, mix with 12 washed, thinly-sliced mushrooms. Serve with French dressing.

TOASTED ROLLS   PINEAPPLE CHUNKS MARINATED IN BANANA LIQUEUR

Spareribs and Sauerkraut Maui

OVEN TIME: 1 HOUR AT 350°   4 SERVINGS

2 pounds spareribs, cut into serving pieces
¼ cup chopped green pepper
¼ cup chopped onion
¼ cup thin celery slices
2 tablespoons bacon fat
1 tablespoons cornstarch
1 No. 2 can pineapple tidbits in sirup
¼ cup vinegar
1 tablespoon soy sauce
1 quart sauerkraut

1. Cook spareribs in boiling salted water. Let simmer for one hour.
2. While ribs cook, sauté green pepper, onion, and celery in hot bacon fat until soft but not brown. Stir in cornstarch. Now add pineapple tidbits and sirup. Cook until thick and clear. Add vinegar and soy sauce.
3. *An hour before serving:* Arrange a layer of sauerkraut in a casserole greased with bacon fat. Add drained spareribs. Pour sauce over all. Put into oven, cover and bake until spareribs are deep brown. Delicious!

party with Hawaiian touches

MINTED FRUIT COCKTAIL   SPARERIBS AND SAUERKRAUT MAUI

SALTED ALMONDS   BAKED SWEET POTATOES   RICE RING

HOT CHEESE BISCUITS   COCONUT LAYER CAKE   ORANGE SHERBET
        ICED TEA

Pork Tenderloin with Prunes

OVEN TIME: 15 MINUTES AT 450°; 2-2½ HOURS AT 350°   8 SERVINGS

4-6 pound pork tenderloin
½ lemon
¾ cup cooked pitted prunes
2 teaspoons salt
¼ teaspoon pepper
1 teaspoon ginger
¼ cup prune juice
¼ cup hot water

1. Preheat oven for about 15 minutes.
2. Wipe pork and rub with lemon. Cut a pocket on long side of meat and stuff it with prunes. Tie with string. Put it into casserole which is just about the same size as the roast.
3. Brown roast on all sides in hot oven. Sprinkle it with salt, pepper, and ginger.
4. Reduce heat to 350°, pour in prune juice and water, cover casserole and continue baking until pork is tender. The flavor is grand!

hearty fare for winter days

PORK TENDERLOIN WITH PRUNES   CAULIFLOWER AND CHEESE CASSE-
ROLE. Cook 1 large head cauliflower until tender. Season with salt and pepper. Make 1 cup white sauce, remove from heat, add ¼ cup grated American cheese. Pour over cauliflower. Sprinkle with crumbs. Bake 15 minutes. Serve right from casserole.

CINNAMON BUNS   BEVERAGE

Chuck Wagon Hot Pots

OVEN TIME: 30 MINUTES AT 375°   6 SERVINGS

6 tart apples, pared and cored
3 cups canned baked beans
6 thick pork chops
2 tablespoons brown sugar
3 tablespoons tomato catsup

Cut apples into thick slices. Divide into 6 well-greased individual casseroles. Spoon beans on top of apples. Wipe chops. Cut off excess fat. Brown on both sides in frying pan on top of stove. Press one chop gently into each bed of beans in each casserole. Sprinkle with brown sugar and tomato catsup. Cover casseroles (use aluminum foil if they do not have lids) and bake until very hot and browned. Serve immediately in individual pots. So easy!

supper after a square dance

CHUCK WAGON HOT POTS   OLD-FASHIONED LETTUCE SALAD. Dice 6 bacon slices. Fry slowly until crisp and brown. Combine bacon pieces with 2 tablespoons bacon fat, 1 tablespoon each of flour and sugar. Cook slowly until smooth. Add ½ cup each vinegar and water. Simmer slowly to make smooth thick sauce. Pour warm dressing over 1 quart crisp washed lettuce and scallion pieces. Serve immediately.
WARM APPLE PIE   COFFEE

Pork Chop and Rice Casserole

OVEN TIME: 1 HOUR AT 375°   4 SERVINGS

4 thick pork chops
1 teaspoon salt
¼ teaspoon pepper
1 package frozen lima beans
½ cup uncooked rice
4 thick tomato slices
4 squares of green pepper
1 cup chicken consommé

Brown chops slowly on one side. Transfer them, browned side up, to greased casserole large enough to hold them in only one layer. Sprinkle with salt and pepper. Break up block of lima beans and put around chops. Spread 2 tablespoons rice over each chop. Now put a tomato slice over each. Season again with salt and pepper. Top with squares of green pepper. Pour chicken consommé along sides of casserole. Cover and bake until chops are tender and rice is fluffy. Practical and popular casserole.

for the main dish

PORK CHOP AND RICE CASSEROLE

OLD-FASHIONED APPLE SLICES. Wash, core and slice 4 large apples. Put into shallow casserole. Dot with 2 tablespoons butter. Combine 1 cup sugar, ½ teaspoons cinnamon, ½ teaspoon nutmeg, ½ cup cream. Pour over apples. Bake ½ hour until apples are tender.

MARVELOUS CHICKEN AND GAME CASSEROLES

Gina's Chicken Cacciatore : Corn and Chicken Potpie : Chicken Tamale Casserole : Chicken Halekulani : Boo Loo Gai : Chicken Paprikas with Rice : Manhattan Chicken Barbecue : Casserole of Chicken, Peas, and Carrots : Coq au Vin : Carolina Jumbalaya : Paella Valenciana : Chicken à la Russe : East Indian Chicken Curry : Chicken Demidoff : Chicken and Ham Gourmet : Champagne Chicken Casserole : Chicken Puff Louise : Chicken Gumbo Casserole : Chicken Salad Casserole : Chicken Tetrazzini : Old-Fashioned Chicken Pie : Quick Chicken and Oyster Casserole : Honolulu Chicken Livers and Rice : Divine Duckling with Orange Sauce : Duck, Peas and Mushrooms in Burgundy : Turkey Monte Carlo : Turkey and Macaroni en Casserole : Cornish Hen Smitane

Gina's Chicken Cacciatore

OVEN TIME: 1½ HOURS AT 325°   4 SERVINGS

1 cut-up broiling chicken, about 3 pounds
2 cloves garlic, minced or pressed
¼ cup olive oil
1 teaspoon paprika
½ cup finely chopped onion
3 cups canned tomatoes
1 teaspoon salt
¼ teaspoon pepper
¼ teaspoon dried rosemary
½ cup dry white wine
¼ cup brandy

Brown chicken and garlic in a heavy saucepan in hot olive oil. Sprinkle chicken with paprika as it browns to enhance color. Discard garlic. Transfer browned chicken to medium casserole. Add onion, tomatoes, salt, pepper, rosemary, wine and brandy to saucepan. Bring to boil. Pour over chicken. Cover casserole and bake until chicken is tender, and sauce thick. Easy to reheat this recipe, so make double the quantity and freeze half. Such compliments as this will get!

a favorite dinner

DRY SHERRY   CHEESE AND CRACKER TRAY

GINA'S CHICKEN CACCIATORE   COOKED SPAGHETTI

PINEAPPLE RICE PUDDING. Separate 2 eggs. Combine yolks with 1½ cups cooked rice, 1 cup crushed canned pineapple, ½ cup pineapple sirup, ½ cup sugar, 1 cup milk, ½ teaspoon vanilla. Fold in stiffly beaten egg whites. Put into buttered medium casserole and bake 20 minutes.   BEVERAGE

Corn and Chicken Potpie

OVEN TIME: 35-45 MINUTES AT 425°   6-8 SERVINGS

3 cups cooked chicken, cut into large pieces
1 can condensed cream of chicken soup
1½ cups milk
½ cup flour
2 egg yolks, slightly beaten
2 cups packaged biscuit mix
2 tablespoons butter or margarine
¼ cup chopped parsley
2 egg whites, stiffly beaten
½ teaspoon salt
¼ cup flour
1 No. 303 can cream-style corn

1. Turn chicken into greased large casserole.
2. Combine chicken soup, milk and flour. Simmer until thickened. Pour over chicken.
3. Stir egg yolks into biscuit mix. Add enough cold water to make stiff dough. Roll out on floured board to 9x12 inches. Spread with butter and parsley. Roll up like jelly roll starting with long side. Cut into twelve 1-inch slices.
4. Combine salt, flour and corn. Fold into beaten egg whites and spread on top of chicken.
5. Arrange biscuit rolls around edge of dish. Bake in hot oven until puffy and brown.

summer story

CORN AND CHICKEN POTPIE   MELON BALLS AND SEEDLESS GRAPES
HOT BISCUITS   RASPBERRY TARTS   CHILLED BEVERAGE

Chicken Halekulani

OVEN TIME: 35-45 MINUTES AT 350°   4 SERVINGS

2 cups shredded packaged coconut
1 cup milk
1 broiling chicken, about 2½ pounds, opened flat and boned
Salt and pepper
2 tablespoons butter
1 large spear of fresh pineapple
¼ cup milk
½ cup seasoned flour
3 cups velouté sauce (a medium white sauce but made
    with chicken stock rather than milk)
2 egg yolks, slightly beaten

(Adapted from a recipe given to me by Mr. William Kelley of
the Halekulani Hotel in Honolulu. It is less complicated than
appears—and unusually good.)

1. Soak 1 cup coconut in 1 cup milk for about 1 hour. Simmer
10 minutes. Cool. Strain through cheesecloth to extract all liquid. Reserve this coconut milk.
2. Toast ½ cup shredded coconut in hot oven. Reserve toasted
and untoasted coconut.
3. Wipe chicken with damp cloth. Season with salt and pepper.
Dot with butter.
4. Put pineapple spear (from fresh pineapple) in center, and
roll chicken into neat bundle. Tie securely with thread at both
ends and in the middle.
5. Dip rolled chicken in milk, dredge in seasoned flour.

6. Make sauce: Cook down velouté to 2 cups. Combine with egg yolks. Heat slowly until it is about to reach boiling point. Remove from flame.
7. Coat chicken with sauce; roll in toasted coconut chips; sauté in hot butter.
8. Transfer chicken to casserole.
9. Add coconut milk to pan in which chicken was sautéed, stirring to pick up all the bits that cling to pan. Pour over chicken, top with reserved coconut meat, cover casserole and bake until chicken is tender. Serve with cooked rice, bananas baked with sugar (same time as chicken), orange and lemon juice. Salad of watercress, cooked spinach, chopped onion, dressing.

For 8 people, double quantities and plan on buffet service. Use a pale green cloth; border with lacy fern or ti leaves. Make an arrangement of colorful tropical fruits and brilliant flowers in woven or wooden containers. As a centerpiece, prepare watermelon boat. Cut off top of melon, lengthwise. Scoop out fruit with melon ball cutter. Combine drained watermelon balls with grapes, cantaloupe balls, and other seasonal fruits. Refrigerate until just before you announce dinner, then serve as first course.

in an Hawaiian mood

CHICKEN HALEKULANI. A glorious dish!   SPINACH SALAD. Wash 1 pound spinach. Using tender leaves only, tear into shreds. Toss with 1 bunch chopped watercress. Serve with French dressing, to which you have added 1 tablespoon finely chopped onion.
CRUNCHY RICE. If you have a chafing dish, cook rice at the table or keep it warm over hot water. Combine 1½ cups raw rice with 3½ cups boiling salted water or chicken consommé. Cook 20 minutes or so until soft. Stir in butter, and just before serving add several tablespoons of chopped blanched almonds or walnuts.
FRUIT PLATTER with whipped cream cheese and sugared crushed berries.   PINEAPPLE CAKE   ICED COFFEE OR TEA

Chicken Tamale Casserole

OVEN TIME: 35 MINUTES AT 375°   6 SERVINGS

1 tablespoon olive oil
1 onion, minced
1 clove garlic, minced
2 cups chicken stock or consommé
1 teaspoon salt
¼ cup tomato paste
1½ cups canned tomatoes
½ cup chopped black olives
½ cup yellow corn meal
1½ teaspoon chili powder
2 cups cooked chicken, cut into bite-size pieces

Heat oil, add onion and garlic, and cook until soft and yellow. Stir in chicken stock, salt, tomato paste, canned tomatoes, olives, corn meal and chili powder. Cook slowly about 15 minutes until thickened. Combine with chicken, then spoon into casserole. Bake uncovered until oozing and nicely browned. (If mixture gets too thick to spoon, thin with hot chicken stock or water.)

memorable meal

CHICKEN TAMALE PIE   AVOCADO AND FRUIT SALAD. Peel 3 small avocados and cut in small dice. Add 1 tablespoon grated onion, 1 cup chopped pitted dates, and 1 cup diced peeled orange sections. Serve in individual plates in lettuce cups.
LEMON CHIFFON PIE   BEVERAGE

Boo Loo Gai

OVEN TIME: ABOUT 1 HOUR AT 350°   8 SERVINGS

2 broiling chickens, each 3 pounds
4 tablespoons peanut oil
2 green peppers cut into 1-inch squares
1 cup pineapple sirup
1 cup pineapple tidbits
½ cup soy sauce
2 tablespoons sugar
1 teaspoon garlic salt
¼ teaspoon pepper

Wipe and dry chicken. Brown in hot oil with green peppers. Put into shallow casserole. Combine other ingredients, pour into casserole, cover and bake until chicken is fork tender. Serve with hot rice. If Chinese cooking appeals to you, you'll surely like this.

Oriental dinner for eight

BOO LOO GAI   CURRIED RICE CASSEROLE. Combine 4 cups cooked rice (1 generous cup when uncooked) with 2 cups chicken stock or bouillon cubes dissolved in hot water. Add ½ cup chopped tomatoes, 1 teaspoon salt, ½ small chopped onion, 2 tablespoons melted butter and 1 teaspoon curry powder. Bake in greased casserole for 30 minutes. Do not bake longer or it will get too dry.   DEEP FRIED ALMONDS
FRUIT PLATTER   BUTTER COOKIES   CHINESE TEA

Chicken Paprikas with Rice

OVEN TIME: 1½ HOURS AT 325°   6-8 SERVINGS

1 cut-up roasting chicken, 4-5 pounds
¼ cup seasoned flour (salt and pepper added to flour)
3 tablespoons fat or lard
1 cup chopped onions
Boiling water (about 1 quart)
1 cup uncooked rice
1 teaspoon salt
½ teaspoon paprika
1 cup commercial sour cream

Shake chicken, 2 or 3 pieces at a time, in a paper bag with flour. Melt fat in large skillet, and cook onions lightly but do not brown them. Push onions to one side and now brown chicken, turning once. Pour in boiling water to cover. Add rice, salt and paprika (more of this if you wish) cover and cook half an hour. Turn into greased 2½-quart casserole, and bake until chicken is fork tender. Remove cover for last 15 minutes so most of gravy is absorbed and top is lightly browned. Stir in sour cream and serve very hot. How savory these Hungarian dishes can be!

supper in a Gypsy mood

CHICKEN PAPRIKAS WITH RICE   CASSEROLE OF CAULIFLOWER AND PEAS. Cook 1 package each frozen peas and cauliflower in boiling salted water 1 inch deep. When tender, put into casserole with 1 cup white sauce to which you have added 1 slightly beaten egg yolk. Cover with buttered bread crumbs. Bake uncovered until crusty and brown (half an hour).   YEAST BREAD

APPLE STRUDEL   BEVERAGE

Manhattan Chicken Barbecue

OVEN TIME: ABOUT 1¼ HOURS AT 350°   8 SERVINGS

2 quartered broiling chickens, each 3 pounds
1 cup water
2 teaspoons salt
1 teaspoon pepper
2 tablespoons paprika
2 tablespoons sugar
1 cup chopped onions
2 cups tomato puree
½ cup oil or fat
½ cup lemon juice or vinegar
1½ tablespoons Worcestershire sauce

Arrange washed chicken pieces in large shallow casserole. In a saucepan, combine water, salt, pepper, paprika, sugar, onions, tomato puree and oil. Bring to boil, then remove from heat. Stir in lemon juice or vinegar, and Worcestershire sauce. Pour half of sauce over chicken. Cover casserole and bake about ¾ hour. Uncover casserole, add remaining sauce and bake uncovered 20 minutes longer or until chicken is fork tender and juicy.

let's have a barbecue

MANHATTAN CHICKEN BARBECUE   OVEN ROAST CORN. Remove silk and tough outer husks from corn, but leave inner husks. Butter. Put in oven to bake for 25-30 minutes.   ANCHOVY TOSSED SALAD. Tear washed crisp head of endive, Boston and watercress. Combine with ¼ cup chopped celery and 2 tablespoons chopped parsley. Toss with ½ cup French dressing. Arrange 12 anchovy strips on top.
TOASTED RYE BREAD   BEVERAGE

Casserole of Chicken, Peas, and Carrots

BAKING TIME: 1 HOUR AT 350°   2-4 SERVINGS

1 cut-up broiling chicken, 2-3 pounds
¼ cup seasoned flour
2 tablespoons bacon fat or oil
1½ cups sliced carrots, partly cooked or frozen
2 cups large green peas, canned or frozen
1 cup water
1 can undiluted mushroom soup
1 teaspoon Worcestershire sauce
Salt and pepper
3 bacon slices

Shake chicken, 2 or 3 pieces at a time, in a paper bag with seasoned flour (½ teaspoon salt, dash of pepper). Quickly brown in hot fat, turning once. In a greased shallow casserole, arrange a layer of chicken, a layer of carrots, and a layer of peas. Repeat layers. To the pan in which chicken was fried, add water, mushroom soup, and Worcestershire. Bring to quick boil, stirring to pick up the little pieces which cling to the pan. Add salt and pepper to taste. Pour over chicken. Top with bacon. Cover and bake until chicken is tender enough to eat with a spoon.

a little dinner

CASSEROLE OF CHICKEN, PEAS AND CARROTS   SCALLOPED POTATOES.
Cut 2 uncooked pared potatoes into thin slices. Put into small buttered casserole. Season with salt and pepper. Combine 2 tablespoons butter, 1 tablespoon flour and 1½ cups milk. Pour over potatoes. Bake uncovered 1 hour.
SLICED TOMATOES   BUTTERED POPCORN   FRUIT TARTS   COFFEE

Coq au Vin

OVEN TIME: 1½ HOURS AT 325°   6 SERVINGS

2 cut-up chickens, each 2½ pounds
6 tablespoons butter
2 cloves garlic, finely minced or crushed
1 dozen small white onions
1 cup sliced mushrooms
¼ cup brandy
2 cups Burgundy wine
1 teaspoon salt
¼ teaspoon pepper
1 teaspoon chopped parsley
Dash of thyme and cloves
1 bay leaf, crumpled

This is one of the most famous of all French casserole dishes. If made a day ahead and warmed in a moderate oven for half an hour before serving, it tastes even better. In a large ovenproof casserole, put chicken, butter, garlic, onions and mushrooms. Brown slowly on top of stove, turning until all the chicken pieces are golden. Pour the brandy over the chicken and set it aflame. Extinguish the blaze by adding wine. Season with salt, pepper, parsley, thyme, cloves, and bay leaf. Cover casserole and bake until done. Serve with crisp hot French bread and a bottle of good red Burgundy wine.

winter dinner

COQ AU VIN   ENDIVE AND CHIVE SALAD. Wash 6 endives, cut in half
    lengthwise. Sprinkle with 2 tablespoons chopped chives or
    scallions. Chill. Just before serving, cover with French dressing.
BURGUNDY WINE   CRISP FRENCH BREAD   FRUIT BASKET   COFFEE

Carolina Jumbalaya

OVEN TIME: 1 HOUR AT 350°   8 SERVINGS

3 slices bacon, minced
1 cup finely chopped onion
1 cup finely chopped green pepper
2 cloves garlic, finely chopped
1½ cups diced cooked chicken
1½ cups diced cooked ham
2 cups tomatoes, cooked or canned
1 cup uncooked rice
2½ cups chicken stock
½ teaspoon thyme
1 bay leaf
Dash of cayenne pepper
1 teaspoon salt

1. Preheat oven.
2. Fry bacon in skillet. Add onion, green pepper and garlic.
Cook slowly until tender, turning often so onions do not burn.
3. Add chicken and ham, and sauté 10 minutes longer.
4. Put in other ingredients. Taste. Season with more cayenne
(or chili powder) if you want a hotter taste. Turn into greased
large casserole. Bake in preheated oven until rice is tender and
most of liquid is absorbed.

deep South supper

CAROLINA JUMBALAYA   HOT GREEN BEANS
BUTTERED BISCUITS   PECAN PIE   COFFEE

Paella Valenciana

OVEN TIME: 1-1½ HOURS AT 350°   6 SERVINGS

1 cut-up roasting chicken, about 5 pounds
4 tablespoons olive oil
3 garlic cloves, finely minced or crushed
2 cups chopped onions
2 cups raw rice
3 cups boiling chicken stock
12 thin slices Spanish or Italian sausage
24 clams, shucked
24 shrimps, shelled
Salt and pepper
3 threads Spanish saffron
3 tablespoons shredded pimentos

1. Wipe chicken pieces. Brown in hot oil in large flameproof casserole with garlic and onions. Turn to cook on all sides.
2. Add rice and chicken stock, and bring to boil.
3. Now add sausage slices, clams, shrimps, salt, pepper, and saffron and bring to boil once again. Cover casserole and place in oven. Bake slowly until chicken is tender and rice is done. Add chicken stock from time to time if needed.
4. Sprinkle with pimentos and serve hot.

Some of the ingredients may be omitted, but the taste is richer if you use all. To stretch this dish, add other varieties of fish and shellfish such as lobster, crabmeat, mussels, and fresh cod.

Chicken à La Russe

1 cut-up broiling chicken, about 3 pounds
½ cup seasoned flour (½ teaspoon salt, ¼ teaspoon each pepper and paprika)
¼ cup fat
1 medium onion, finely chopped
1 clove garlic, finely chopped
¼ cup coarsely chopped blanched almonds
3 tablespoons flour
1½ cups cooked or canned tomatoes
1 tablespoon tomato paste
2 cups chicken stock or bouillon
¾ cup commercial sour cream

Shake chicken (2 or 3 pieces at a time) in a paper bag with seasoned flour. Heat fat in skillet and brown chicken pieces, turning to cook all sides evenly. Transfer the browned pieces to a buttered medium casserole. Add onion, garlic, and almonds to the skillet and cook gently until the almonds are brown and the onions soft and clear but not brown. Gently stir in the flour and cook 2 or 3 minutes. Add tomatoes, tomato paste and chicken stock or bouillon. Cook, stirring frequently, until the mixture boil and begins to thicken. Remove from heat. Slowly stir in sour cream. Pour sauce into casserole, cover and cook in oven until chicken is fork tender. A richly flavored casserole.

company buffet

CHILLED BORSHT WITH CUCUMBER SLICES. Buy bottled borsht or use tomato juice.

CHICKEN À LA RUSSE	BUTTERED COOKED NOODLES
WHOLE WHEAT ROLLS	FRESH FRUIT COFFEE

East Indian Chicken Curry

OVEN TIME: 1 HOUR AT 325°   4 SERVINGS

1 cut-up broiling chicken, about 3 pounds
2 tablespoons oil
1 large green pepper, chopped
1 clove garlic, finely minced
½ cup chopped onions
2 cups cooked or canned tomatoes
1 teaspoon curry powder (more for a stronger curry)
½ teaspoon thyme
1 teaspoon salt
½ teaspoon pepper
2 cups cooked rice
4 tablespoons seedless raisins
⅓ cup blanched almonds

Wash and dry chicken. Heat oil in skillet and brown pieces on all sides. Place them in a medium casserole as they get done. To skillet, add green pepper, garlic, and onions. Cook gently for 3 minutes, stirring frequently. Add tomatoes, curry, thyme, salt and pepper, rice, and half the raisins. Simmer 15 minutes, then pour over chicken in casserole. Cover and cook until largest pieces are tender. Sprinkle with remaining raisins and almonds and serve from casserole. A wonderful curry that is not too hot for most tastes.

for a neighborhood "sociable"

EAST INDIAN CHICKEN CURRY   CURRY ACCOMPANIMENTS. Arrange in small bowls several of the following: crumbled crisp cooked bacon, chopped green onions, chutney, salted peanuts, candied ginger, preserved kumquats, grated coconut, chopped hard-cooked eggs, fried onion rings.

CRISP CRACKERS   WARM APPLE PIE   CHEESE   COFFEE

Chicken Demidoff

OVEN TIME: ABOUT 1 HOUR AT 350°   4 SERVINGS

1 quartered broiling chicken, about 3 pounds
¼ cup butter
1 cup sliced carrots, cut 1 inch thick
½ cup turnips, cut into balls
½ cup celery, cut into ½-inch pieces
½ cup small onions, cut into thin slices
½ cup mushrooms, cut into thin slices
1 teaspoon salt
¼ teaspoon pepper
½ cup chicken stock or bouillon cubes dissolved in water

Brown chicken on all sides in hot butter. Transfer to greased small casserole. Briefly sauté each vegetable separately in the hot butter. Season with salt and pepper. Arrange vegetables around chicken in alternate groups. Pour in chicken stock. Cover casserole and bake in moderate oven until everything is tender. Uncover for last 15 minutes to brown top.

little dinner gem

CHICKEN DEMIDOFF   GRAPEFRUIT SALAD. Combine 2 cups grapefruit sections (no membranes please), ¼ cup chopped green pepper, 3 tablespoons chopped pimentos, 1 cup peeled, cored and diced apples, ½ cup chopped walnuts. Mix with honey and lemon juice. Serve in clean grapefruit shells in a bed of lettuce.

DINNER ROLLS   FRUIT TARTS   COFFEE

Chicken and Ham Gourmet

OVEN TIME: ABOUT 1 HOUR AT 375°   4 SERVINGS

6 thin slices cooked ham
1 cut-up broiling chicken, 3-4 pounds
¼ cup butter
1 cup carrots cut into ½-inch slices
1 cup potato balls (cut with melon scoop)
½ cup thinly sliced onions
½ cup thinly sliced celery
2 cups canned button mushrooms, drained
1½ teaspoons salt
¼ teaspoon pepper
1 cup chicken stock

1. Line a greased oval casserole with ham slices.
2. Brown the chicken on top of the stove in hot butter. Transfer to casserole, leaving as much butter in saucepan as possible.
3. In butter left in saucepan, sauté the vegetables. Put them around the chicken in the casserole.
4. Bring chicken stock to quick boil in saucepan, and let cook for 5 minutes until it is somewhat reduced. Pour reduced stock into casserole, cover and bake until chicken is tender. Dust with paprika before serving.

elegant supper

CHICKEN AND HAM GOURMET   SALAD. Arrange separated leaves of endive on chilled salad plates, spoke fashion, with points at outer edge of plate. Sprinkle paper thin slices of radishes and celery over leaves. Cover with 3 tablespoons grated cheese. Serve with French dressing.

TOASTED VIENNA LOAF   BLACK CHERRIES IN COINTREAU   BEVERAGE

Champagne Chicken Casserole

OVEN TIME: 30-35 MINUTES AT 350°   6 SERVINGS

6 breasts of chicken (if frozen, thaw before cooking)
¼ cup seasoned flour (1 teaspoon salt and a dash of pepper)
5 tablespoons butter
1 cup sliced mushrooms
1 onion, finely chopped
30 small potato balls (cut out with potato ball cutter or
    melon scoop)
1 cup champagne
1 cup cream sauce (made with chicken stock and cream,
    instead of water and milk)

Shake chicken in a paper bag with seasoned flour. Sauté in hot butter until golden on both sides. Transfer to elegant buttered casserole. In same saucepan, sauté first mushrooms, then onion, then potatoes. Surround chicken with vegetables. Pour in champagne (save a few tablespoons for later) and cream sauce. Cover casserole and bake until chicken is tender. Remove cover for last 10 minutes. Take casserole from oven, stir in remaining champagne and serve to your favorite people.

for a sparkling evening

CHAMPAGNE CHICKEN CASSEROLE   SALAD OF HEART OF PALM OR
    ENDIVE   FRENCH DRESSING
CHILLED CHAMPAGNE. Not iced.   FRESH UNHULLED STRAWBERRIES.
    Chill them. Serve with a mound of sugar and cream.

Chicken Puff Louise

OVEN TIME: 40-50 MINUTES AT 375°   6 SERVINGS

1 can condensed cream of mushroom soup
⅓ cup milk
1½ cups cubed cooked chicken
1½ cups cooked green beans, drained
4 eggs, separated
¼ cup shredded American cheese

1. Preheat oven for 8 or 10 minutes.
2. Combine soup and milk in 1½-quart casserole.
3. Stir in chicken and green beans. Bake for 10 minutes.
4. Meanwhile beat egg yolks well, add cheese. Beat egg whites until stiff. Fold into egg-cheese mixture.
5. Pile egg topping on hot chicken and continue baking for half an hour or so. An elegant little luncheon dish.

guest luncheon or supper

CHICKEN PUFF LOUISE. Each bite is a delicious morsel.

SHRIMP, ALMOND AND CELERY SALAD. Clean and cook 1½ pounds shrimp in boiling water with a bay leaf, tablespoon dry mustard, and vinegar. Cool in same water. Chop shrimp coarsely. Put 1 pound blanched almonds, and 1 bunch washed celery separately through food chopper. Put 4 hardcooked eggs through ricer. Mix all ingredients with mayonnaise and salt to taste. Serve chilled on lettuce.

WARM CLOVERLEAF ROLLS   COFFEE

CHICKEN & GAME   113

Chicken Gumbo Casserole

OVEN TIME: 20-25 MINUTES AT 375°   6 SERVINGS

1 cup diced cooked chicken
1 cup diced cooked ham
2 cups cooked rice
1 can of chicken gumbo soup
2 tablespoons chopped pimento
6 slices canned pineapple, drained
6 teaspoons brown sugar
3 tablespoons melted butter
18 cloves

Combine chicken, ham, rice, soup, and pimento and put into greased medium casserole. Sprinkle pineapple with brown sugar and melted butter. Stick 3 cloves into each one. Top chicken mixture with spiced pineapple rings and bake uncovered until pineapple is glazed. There's excellent flavor in this simple casserole.

dinner for six

CHICKEN GUMBO CASSEROLE   SWEET POTATO CASSEROLE. Beat until fluffy 6 cooked sweet potatoes with 3 tablespoons butter and ¼ cup cream. Add ¼ cup sherry, salt and pepper. Transfer to greased casserole. Bake 20 minutes.   SLICED TOMATOES
HOT POPOVERS   ICE CREAM WITH ROAST GROUND PEANUTS   COFFEE

Chicken Salad Casserole

2 cups diced cooked chicken
1½ cups celery, diced
¼ cup toasted almonds, chopped
2 teaspoons finely chopped onion
1 tablespoon lemon juice
Dash of pepper
⅔ cup salad dressing
1 teaspoon salt
1 cup (¼ pound) snappy American cheese
¾ cup crushed potato chips

Combine chicken, celery, almonds, onion, lemon juice and pepper in large mixing bowl. Add salad dressing and mix gently but thoroughly. Spoon into 4 individual shallow casseroles. Sprinkle with cheese. Top with potato chips. Heat casseroles until cheese begins to bubble. Serve with crushed pineapple on side.

dinner on the terrace

CHICKEN SALAD CASSEROLE   BAKED RICE. In saucepan, cook 2 sliced onions in butter until soft. Transfer to buttered medium casserole. To saucepan, add 1 cup uncooked rice, a 10-ounce can chicken consomme (or bouillon cubes dissolved in water) and 1 cup water. Bring to boil. Cook gently for 15 minutes. Sprinkle with salt and pepper to taste. Bake. Transfer to casserole ½ hour until liquid is absorbed.

POPOVERS   CHEESE CAKE   WATERMELON   COFFEE

Chicken Tetrazzini

OVEN TIME: ABOUT ½ HOUR AT 375°   6 SERVINGS

4 tablespoons butter
½ cup chopped onion
¼ cup chopped green pepper
1 cup sliced mushrooms, fresh or canned
4 tablespoons flour
1½ cups milk
1 cup sauterne wine
1 tablespoon Worcestershire sauce
1 teaspoon salt
¼ teaspoon pepper
1½ cups cooked chicken (preferably all white meat), cut
    into bite-size pieces
2 cups cooked thin spaghetti
1 cup grated American cheese

Melt butter, sauté onion, pepper and mushrooms until soft. Stir in flour, now add milk, wine, Worcestershire, salt and pepper. Cook slowly for 10 minutes until thickened. Add chicken and spaghetti and half of cheese. Put into greased medium casserole. Top with remaining cheese. Cover and bake until bubbly hot.

company luncheon

CHICKEN TETRAZZINI   SPINACH AND CREAM CASSEROLE. Wash thoroughly 2 pounds spinach. Cook until soft. Put through food chopper using fine grind. Drain. Put spinach into small buttered casserole with salt, pepper, ¼ pound butter. Bake until dry. Stir in ¾ cup cream. Put back in oven until cream is heated. Most delicious!

BLUEBERRY MUFFINS   COFFEE

Old-Fashioned Chicken Pie

BAKING TIME: 20-30 MINUTES AT 425°   6-8 SERVINGS

1 stewing chicken, about 5 pounds, cut into pieces
Pastry for 2-crust pie, seasoned with rosemary
1½ teaspoons dried rosemary
3 tablespoons flour
1 egg yolk, beaten slightly
Salt and pepper
½ cup cooked peas
½ cup cooked carrots
½ cup cooked pearl onions

1. *Early in the day:* Cover cleaned chicken with boiling salted water and simmer until tender. Time will vary with age of fowl, but allow at least 2½ hours.
2. Meanwhile, make a pastry crust from your favorite recipe or using a quick mix. Cut in rosemary with the shortening when you are making the crust. Roll it to fit the top of the casserole (you will need one with a capacity of about 2½ quarts). Reserve unbaked crust.
3. Remove chicken as soon as tender, bone and cut into large pieces.
4. Boil stock rapidly until reduced to 2½ cups. Stir in flour and egg yolk to thicken. Add salt and pepper to taste.
5. *40 minutes before serving:* Preheat oven. Gently combine chicken pieces, peas, carrots, onions, and thickened stock. Pour into large casserole. Top with pastry, pressing down on sides. Cut gashes on top so steam can escape.
6. Bake in hot oven until crust is brown. A complete meal with chicken, vegetables, and pastry in one dish.

Quick Chicken and Oyster Casserole

OVEN TIME: 15-20 MINUTES AT 375°   6 SERVINGS

2 cups cooked diced chicken
1 pint oysters
2 cups thin cream sauce (made with chicken stock and
    cream instead of water)
½ cup buttered crushed cracker crumbs

Spoon the chicken into a greased 1½-quart casserole, piling it in the middle. Surround with oysters. Pour in the cream sauce, top with crumbs, and bake uncovered until oysters are plump. Or bake and serve in individual ramekins or casseroles. Good with mushrooms and tomatoes. Quick but delicious, this is a company dish—the kind that lets you spend more time with them and less in the kitchen.

easy buffet for six

A simple but good supper for the hostess who likes to relax even when company is coming.

QUICK CHICKEN AND OYSTER CASSEROLE   TOSSED SALAD. Wash and store in refrigerator in damp towel an assortment of salad greens—endive, chicory, romaine, Boston, endive, parsley, chives. Mix in big bowl at the table with French dressing to which you have added a hint of Tabasco.

RYE KRISP   PEPPERMINT ICE CREAM WITH CHOCOLATE CHIPS
    BEVERAGE

Honolulu Chicken Livers and Rice

1 cup raw rice
3 cups boiling chicken stock or water
½ cup canned mushrooms (or fresh ones sautéed in butter)
1 pound chicken livers
½ teaspoon salt
¼ teaspoon pepper
¼ cup molasses

Cook rice in boiling chicken stock or water for 20 minutes. Stir in mushrooms. Spread half of mixture into a buttered small casserole. Wipe livers. Cut in half. Season them with salt and pepper and dip into molasses. Transfer to casserole on top of rice. Add remaining rice and mushrooms, cover casserole and bake until livers are tender, rice is fluffy, and sauce is thick and delicious.

luncheon for company

HONOLULU CHICKEN LIVERS AND RICE   PINEAPPLE PUDDING. Cream ⅓ cup butter with ¼ cup sugar. Add 2 beaten egg yolks, 1 cup bread crumbs, 1 cup crushed drained canned pineapple. Fold in 2 beaten egg whites. Turn into buttered casserole and bake 35 minutes.

ASPARAGUS SALAD. Serve cooked asparagus tips on shredded romaine lettuce, with mayonnaise mixed with chopped fresh parsley or dill.

TOASTED CINNAMON BREAD   COFFEE

Divine Duckling with Orange Sauce

1 quartered duckling, about 4 pounds
Garlic clove
Salt and pepper
8 small white onions

Orange Sauce:
½ cup dry white wine
1 tablespoon sugar
1 teaspoon wine vinegar
1 tablespoon water
¼ teaspoon salt
½ cup orange juice
2 tablespoons lemon juice
2 tablespoons slivered orange rind
1 teaspoon Curaçao or brandy

1. Rub duckling with peeled cut garlic. Sprinkle with salt and pepper. Brown in casserole in hot oven. You will have to turn pieces once or twice to brown all over.
2. Pour off fat, arrange orange slices on duck; border with onions. Cover casserole. Reduce heat to 350 and bake 1 hour longer or until duck is tender. Discard discolored orange slices.
3. Make sauce: Remove juices from casserole, skimming off fat. Add juices to wine. Cook sugar and vinegar in small saucepan until caramel is formed. Stir in wine mixture and water, salt, orange and lemon juices. Boil for 10 minutes. Add orange rind and Curaçao.
4. Pour sauce over duckling and serve at once.

Duck, Peas and Mushrooms in Burgundy

OVEN TIME: 1½ HOURS AT 325°   4-6 SERVINGS

1 cut-up duck, about 4 pounds
¼ cup seasoned flour
2 tablespoons fat
½ pound sliced mushrooms
1 medium onion, chopped
2 cups Burgundy wine (or any dry red wine)
3 cups cooked rice
1 package frozen peas
3 tablespoons shredded pimentos

Choose duck which is not too fat. Shake pieces in paper bag with seasoned flour. Brown in hot fat. Put duck into greased 3-quart casserole. Sauté mushrooms and onions in 2 tablespoons of the fat in which duck was browned. Transfer to casserole. Pour wine over duck. Cover and bake until bird is tender. Test the thickest piece with a fork. Add rice, peas, and pimentos. Cover again and continue baking until peas are done, about 15 minutes. If casserole seems dry, add hot water.

autumn supper

DUCK, PEAS AND MUSHROOMS IN BURGUNDY   BEET, CELERY AND WATERCRESS SALAD. Cut 4 cooked beets into thin slices. Add 1 cup sliced uncooked celery rings and 1 bunch cut-up watercress from which you have removed stems. Serve with French dressing to which you have added 1 teaspoon grated onion.

HOT BUTTERED TOAST   VANILLA ICE CREAM WITH CHOCOLATE SAUCE
COFFEE

Turkey Monte Carlo

OVEN TIME: 15-20 MINUTES AT 350°   4-6 SERVINGS

1 12-ounce package frozen broccoli
2 cups broad noodles
2 tablespoons butter
2 tablespoons flour
1 teaspoon salt
¼ teaspoon black pepper
¼ teaspoon dry mustard
1 cup light cream
1 cup turkey or chicken stock
1 cup grated American cheese
2 cups diced cooked turkey
⅓ cup roasted almonds, slivered

1. Cook broccoli as directed on package. Cook noodles separately. Drain and reserve.
2. Meanwhile make sauce: Melt butter, stir in flour, salt, pepper, and dry mustard. Slowly add cream and chicken stock. (If you do not have stock, use broccoli liquid or water.) Cook, stirring, until thickened. Remove from heat. Add cheese and let it melt.
3. Heat oven. Combine noodles and sauce and turn half into buttered large casserole.
4. Add a layer of turkey and a layer of cooked broccoli. Repeat layers. Finish with remainder of noodles and sauce.
5. Sprinkle with almonds. Bake uncovered until bubbly hot.

holiday buffet

CHILLED MELON BALLS IN CHAMPAGNE. Drink the champagne, then eat the melon.

TURKEY MONTE CARLO   RAW RELISHES

PECAN BISCUITS   PUMPKIN PIE   BEVERAGES

Turkey and Macaroni en Casserole

OVEN TIME: 20 MINUTES AT 350°   4-6 SERVINGS

4 eggs, well beaten
1 cup soft bread crumbs
1 cup (¼ pound) grated American cheese
2 cups diced cooked turkey
2 cups cooked macaroni
2 tablespoons chopped parsley
½ cup finely chopped onion
1 tablespoon chopped pimento
1 teaspoon salt
Dash of pepper
½ teaspoon monosodium glutamate, optional
1½ cups milk
¼ cup butter or margarine

Combine all ingredients except milk and butter. Heat milk, add butter, then pour over first mixture, stirring constantly. Turn into greased 2½-quart casserole. Set in pan of hot water until immersed halfway. Bake in moderate oven until knife inserted in center comes out clean. Serve plain or with mushroom sauce.

November luncheon

Let's be traditional and serve cranberries with turkey, but this year try them in muffins.

TURKEY AND MACARONI EN CASSEROLE   CRANBERRY MUFFINS. To sifted dry ingredients for 12 medium muffins, add ¾ cup chopped uncooked cranberries mixed with ¼ cup sugar. Bake for 20-30 minutes at 425°.   BEVERAGE

Cornish Hen Smitane

OVEN TIME: ABOUT 35 MINUTES AT 350°   4 SERVINGS

Sauce Smitane:
1 cup finely chopped onions
2 teaspoons vinegar
2 cups brown gravy or beef stock
2 tablespoons commercial sour cream
4 tablespoons brandy
1 cup sliced mushrooms
¼ cup seedless raisins
4 whole Cornish hens, about 1¼ pounds each
Salt and pepper
2 tablespoons melted butter
2 tablespoons white wine

I am indebted to M. Rigo Quattrini of New York's famed Restaurant Laurent for this recipe. Cornish hen is a plump-breasted bird which is a cross between game and domestic fowl. Young broilers may be substituted, but they have a blander flavor and less meat.

1. Make the sauce ahead and keep it hot in a double boiler. Or better yet, prepare a day ahead and reheat at the table in a chafing dish. Brown onions in vinegar, add gravy or beef stock and sour cream. Let cook at least one hour.
2. Strain sauce, add brandy, mushrooms, and raisins. Reserve.
3. About 40 minutes before serving, sprinkle birds with salt, pepper, butter and wine. Bake them in oven in covered casserole until tender, about 35 minutes. Turn them several times to baste.
4. Serve each bird over a bed of plain boiled wild rice, and divide hot sauce equally over each one.

Index